aesthetic properties > aesthetic judgment

aesthetic properties + taste

Aesthet
ascrib
+
works

AESTHETIC VALUE

where does aesthetic value reside?

in aesthetic properties of works
(relations of works' base properties
in combinations with each other
+ the ideal observer with taste)

a work's aesthetic properties engage us
fully (cognitively, affectively + perceptually)
and make the work an alternative world

interpretation links
description of base properties to
evaluation + are explanations
seeking to maximise our experience of the
work

the value of art lies in the works
capacity to engage us fully in its alternative
world — pleasure, refreshing, interesting,
emotional

AESTHETIC VALUE

Alan H. Goldman
UNIVERSITY OF MIAMI

WestviewPress

A Division of HarperCollins*Publishers*

Focus Series

Published in 1998 in the United States of America by Westview Press, 5500 Central Avenue, Boulder, Colorado 80301-2877, and in the United Kingdom by Westview Press, 12 Hid's Copse Road, Cumnor Hill, Oxford OX2 9JJ

Library of Congress Cataloging-in-Publication Data
Goldman, Alan H., 1945–
    Aesthetic value / Alan H. Goldman
      p.   cm. — (Focus series)
    Includes bibliographical references and index.
    ISBN 0-8133-2019-4
    1. Aesthetics.   2. Values.   I. Title.   II. Series: Focus series
(Westview Press)
BH39.G5815   1995
111'.85—dc20   95-17025
                                                              CIP

The paper used in this publication meets the requirements of the American
National Standard for Permanence of Paper for Printed Library Materials Z39.48-
1984.

10   9   8   7   6   5   4   3   2   1

For my mother,
who introduced me to music and art,
and for Joan,
who shares the experience of them

CONTENTS

ACKNOWLEDGMENTS

I first thank Stephen Davies for detailed and helpful comments on the entire manuscript. An anonymous referee for Westview also provided some useful criticism. I am grateful to Spencer Carr for providing the incentive to finish this project and thank Sarah Tomasek for making my prose more readable.

Parts of this book have appeared in articles in *The Journal of Philosophy*, *The Journal of Aesthetics and Art Criticism*, *The British Journal of Aesthetics*, and *Philosophy and Phenomenological Research*. I thank those journals for permission to use that material, which has been revised and edited for this book.

Much of the book was written with the help of Orovitz grants from the University of Miami and an NEH summer research grant, for which I am also most grateful.

Alan H. Goldman

CHAPTER ONE

Introduction

The Primacy of Value

Imagine that you are in Paris (always nice to begin a book with a pleasant thought), in the Musée d'Orsay, standing before Whistler's famous portrait of his mother. You are moved by the quiet power of the work, feel its poignancy, and express to yourself surprise that the subdued, almost dull, gray and black colors and the stable, seemingly tranquil forms of the woman seated in profile against the partially curtained wall could have that effect. The nature of this positive evaluation of the work that you have just expressed to yourself is philosophically controversial. It is different from a straightforward judgment of fact, an empirical judgment, because, for one thing, evaluations of artworks are likely to prompt more disagreement from others than straightforward judgments of fact. Your judgment addresses the value in this painting and perhaps expresses your own taste. But although it concerns value, it is not a moral judgment; it does not concern Whistler's behavior toward other persons (which was itself rather controversial). You have made an aesthetic judgment, and the logic of such judgments, how they are alike and different from empirical and moral statements, is a main topic of this book.

Throughout most of its history aesthetics has been concerned with judgments like yours and with the values that can be derived from the appreciation of works of art. That this branch of philosophy should address itself primarily to the evaluation and value of artworks is not surprising. Other branches of philosophy are also concerned in large part with norms or standards of evaluation, whether of claims to knowledge, sound reasoning, or right actions. But the domain of discourse about art is different because judgments about artworks themselves are more often answers to questions about value. In other areas of discourse concern with value is not as central or direct. When we seek empirical knowledge, we try to get hooked up in the right way to independent facts or states of affairs. Although such inquiry is guided by those values it might ultimately serve, empirical judgment itself is not directly a matter of evaluation. Whether something is the case is independent of our wanting or needing it to be so. In contrast to empirical judgment, moral judgment, narrowly construed, is concerned with evaluating actions. But the primary concern here is to censure those acts that are unacceptable to the community because they are incompatible with peaceful and cooperative endeavors. Aesthetic judgments, again by contrast, typically aim to express those positive values that viewers appreciate in artworks.

If you are not a present-day philosopher, your very concept of art is probably evaluative. If you were across town in Paris at the Pompidou Center, you might well wonder whether what's on display is really art. If you did, you would rightly dismiss as irrelevancies the philosopher's recent definitions of art. According to the institutional definition, whatever is on display is necessarily art because it is deemed so in the art world.[1] According to the historical definition, whatever is intended to be viewed as art in the past was properly viewed is necessarily art, again making your question senseless.[2] But your question, which makes perfectly good sense, is why these objects in the Pompidou Center should be on display or should be viewed in the way the Rubens or da Vinci paintings in the Louvre deserve to be viewed. Your concept of art may be grounded in certain accepted paradigms, such as the *Mona Lisa*, but certainly under the assumption that these works are worthy of serious contemplation for the ways they reward such sustained attention. Only an aesthetic theory will make explicit and explain the sources of aesthetic value, but analytic philosophers often forget that the ordinary concept of art, reflected in your bewilderment at some contemporary exhibits, includes implicit reference to this sort of value or valuable experience. Whether there can be bad art (or bad fine art) is at least controversial given the ordinary concept. But even if this category were granted, genuine art should still be intended by its producers or judged by its displayers to afford valuable experience or insight to those who give it their serious attention.

Like the ordinary present-day concept, the traditional philosophical theories or definitions of art (as opposed to the more recent definitions by analytic philosophers) appealed to sources of value in artworks—representation, expression, and formal structure (all of which contribute to the value of the Whistler portrait).[3] Although the theories in question assumed that their central concept referred not only to the central function but also to the primary source of value in art, they did not always meet the burden of explaining why the function in question is valuable. But if the concept of art is an evaluative concept, then there is this burden of explaining how the central features of artworks, whether representational, expressive, or formal, contribute to the values derived from contemplating and appreciating the works. For example, theories of the nature of representation and expression, which abound in contemporary aesthetics, typically try to show how artworks represent objects or express emotion. But they should also show why, if their accounts are correct, these functions of artworks are valuable. A theory of expression that holds that artworks express by arousing emotional states in audiences must indicate why audiences should want such states aroused and why other stimuli that do so should not thereby have equal artistic value. A theory that holds that artworks are expressive not when our emotions are aroused but when we can recognize analogues of emotional states in the works themselves (for example, the resignation in Mrs. Whistler's face) should indicate why such recognition (without engagement of our emotions) should be of any value. Similarly, a theory of representation must show why mere copies of objects should have value beyond that of perceiving the objects themselves, a burden that Plato thought could not be met. And any acceptable theory of art as a whole must account for the importance of art in people's lives, whether that importance derives from the aforementioned features of artworks taken separately or from some other source.

The pervasiveness of evaluative concepts in discourse about art is clear not just from the ordinary concept of art itself but also from the terms we typically use in describing artworks. I have had you describe Whistler's portrait as poignant; you might also say serene, almost devout. Other works in Paris museums might be described as stirring, bold, concise, graceful, true to life; yet others (because there are so many) might be described as insipid, derivative, awkward, groping, loosely woven, and so on. Such terms obviously have an evaluative dimension: They express evaluative responses of viewers to the objective properties of the works described. In general, critics as well will pick out those properties of works that are worth attending to, those that contribute to the positive or negative values of the works. They too will use descriptive terms such as those mentioned, but they will at the same time indicate explicitly those objective properties of the works to which they are responding, so as to guide the perceptions of viewers toward greater appreciation of the works' values.

The objective properties to which one responds when one calls a work tightly knit, poignant, true to life, subtle, or bold are once more formal, expressive, representational, and symbolic features of the work, now together with properties (referred to by such terms as 'bold' or 'original') that relate the work to prior art or artistic traditions (historical properties). This returns us to the problem of explaining how these properties evoke the evaluative responses they do, why they are sources of value for viewers of art. This, as indicated, is no mean task.

Certainly there have been suggestions in the literature of aesthetics. A theory such as Tolstoy's, for example, which views art as a means to communicate or arouse emotions, can cite the human need to communicate feelings, the communal bonds created when emotions are shared, the elevation of spirit when these feelings are of the higher or "religious" kind,[4] or the cathartic effect of experiencing negative emotions from artworks. Nonarousal expressivist theories can hold that we learn about our psychological natures by recognizing analogues of our emotional states in artworks. Formalist theories have tended to emphasize the pleasure derived from the contemplation of beauty or the immediate appeal of "significant form."[5] Suggestions regarding the value of representation have been diverse, including the instinctual enjoyment of imitation (linked to learning), the exemplification of properties that might otherwise go unnoticed and that might lead us to perceive in new ways,[6] the insights to be gained about objects or characters from revealing representations of them, and the formalist suggestion that realistic representation creates a kind of "unity in diversity."[7]

None of these suggestions can be developed into a complete theory of aesthetic value, a theory that indicates a value that great artworks share that is not to be readily found outside art. First, most of them point to an instrumental value of artworks; the feature of art on which they focus is seen as a means to some goal that can be achieved in other ways as well. We communicate feelings, appreciate beauty, teach about objects and persons, and learn about our psyches outside art, and we need to know how art is special in these regards. Surely, there are more direct ways to communicate emotions, for example, and better ways to study psychology. Second, if these features are valuable in the ways described, then artworks that have them should be judged by the degree to which they satisfy these descriptions. They should be better the more beautiful they are, the more lifelike their representations, the more clearly they communicate emotions, and so on. Yet many great works deliberately eschew beauty, distort their representations (Whistler's shapes, for example, are quite flat), or communicate emotions (of the nonreligious variety) subtly and ambiguously. Third, and more obviously, many great artworks lack certain of these features altogether. If we are to find a kind of value that great works of art share, then we cannot do it by trying to construe all music as representational, for example, or all paintings as clearly communicative of particular emotions.

Nevertheless, it must be admitted that some of these features are of value in themselves in particular works and in some of the ways indicated. In the next two chapters I will have more to say about the evaluative aesthetic terms by which we typically describe artworks, the objective properties that ground their correct ascriptions, and the ways in which these properties can be separate sources of value and, more important, can contribute to the overall value of the works that instantiate them. The value of historical properties such as originality, the value of a work that derives from its influences on later works, and in general the problems created for evaluation by relations among works in historical sequences and narratives will require separate treatment in a subsequent chapter.

Interpretation

I mentioned above that critics pick out those features for description that are worth attending to, that contribute to the values of the artworks described. We can say equally that description and attention to particular properties are guided by interpretations of artworks. Critics focus on the features of works that enter their interpretations as explananda (elements to be explained) or explanans (elements of explanations). This equation suggests a theory of interpretation that will be spelled out and defended in Chapter 4.

All interpretation in any domain aims at understanding, and understanding in art and elsewhere requires explanation. To interpret a feature of a work of art is to explain why it is present there. Why, for example, did Whistler place light flecks in the dark curtains or highlight the old woman's hand? In answering these questions an interpreter shows how these features contribute to the overall value of the work. Thus understanding a work of art is being able to appreciate its artistic values. Interpretations that produce such understanding aim to enhance the values of artworks for those audiences who follow them, whose understanding and perception are guided by them. An explanation of how some formal or representational property of a work contributes to its aesthetic value will produce understanding of why that property is present in the work, will guide attention to that property and its relations to others in the work, and will enhance appreciation of the values to which it contributes. Such are the functions of interpretations.

Since different and sometimes incompatible values can be realized by the same artworks under different interpretations, there can be incompatible but equally acceptable interpretations of the same works. A literary work such as *The Turn of the Screw* might afford greater psychological insight under one interpretation but be more expressive or atmospheric under another. If interpretation aimed at truth, if it were a form of empirical inquiry, then the claim of equally acceptable but incompatible interpretations would be incoherent. But interpretation instead links descriptions of artworks to their evaluations, aiming not at truth but at enhancing appreciation of the works they explain. To limit always the acceptable interpretations of an artwork to one would be to deprive audiences guided by them of potential values in the work. Such values are the goal of aesthetic appreciation.

An Overarching Value

Interpretations link descriptions to evaluations. Following the chapters on the description and interpretation of artworks will be a chapter on the values and evaluations at which the former aim. I hinted above that the importance of art in people's lives might be explained by a kind of value that great artworks share across their very different media.[8] This thesis is highly controversial, although implicitly endorsed by some of the best writings in the history of aesthetics. Many contemporary aestheticians would claim instead that an inquiry into aesthetic value should limit itself to a particular art form or era, that we should not expect the benefits derived from reading *Moby Dick* to be at all similar to what we might gain in the experience of listening to a Haydn symphony or viewing the Sistine Chapel.

It can be claimed more narrowly that not only each artistic medium but also each style within an art form sets its own problems and ideals that determine success or failure for works within that style. There is much truth to this claim, and I will make use of it later in discussing problems of evaluation across historical eras. Nor do I want to claim that all art shares the same values or serves the same functions. The concept is too broad for that idea to be plausible. But if the ideals and goals of specific genres are open to criticism, if it is more than an accident of history and language that various art forms are grouped together under the evaluative concept of fine arts (and if this grouping is not based on an obvious mistake such as thinking that all music is representational), if terms we use for representational, formal, and expressive properties are applied across different media, then it is not implausible that at least many great works or paradigms share a kind of value that in large part explains the importance of art for many people. This value ought to be also more or less unique to art if its importance cannot be explained by features it has in common with many other institutions and kinds of objects. Finally, an explanation of this value ought to indicate at the same time how many great works are best perceived and appreciated.

If the primary value we seek is shared by many great artworks but more or less unique to art, then some of the sources of value of particular works and forms mentioned earlier are ruled out of this category. Certain novels, for example, teach us much about history, psychology, and ethics, but their doing so is not something they share with symphonies that might equally explain the importance of both types of artworks. Likewise, the tight and well-defined structures of classical symphonies would find only loose analogues in most good novels. Since not all artworks are representational or clearly expressive of emotion, these separate sources of value for particular types of works cannot be the primary target of our present inquiry either. At the same time, they cannot be ignored as main contributors to the values of many great works. One problem, then, is how to acknowledge these value-producing features of great artworks without overemphasizing their separate contributions. I will argue that our answer lies in the ways that these separate sources of value interact in relating different elements within works. This interaction creates fully engaging and intensely significant experience of these elements and works.

Elements or parts of artworks, whether spatial, temporal, or otherwise, become significant when perceived in terms of their relations to other parts of the works. When these are related via form, representation, expression, or symbol, and when it is further recognized, for example, how form determines representation and representation determines expression in a work, all this makes for an experience or appreciation of the elements of the work that is cognitively, perceptually, and affectively very rich. Recognition of such interaction also generates a different understanding of the separate sources of value we have discussed. Visual representation, for example, can now be appreciated for the way that it allows perceivers to grasp and relate larger spatial units within paintings, facilitating appreciation of formal structure. It is also, of course, a bearer of symbolic content and method of expression.

When all our faculties are so fully absorbed in the attempt to appreciate a great work of art, it is natural for us to view the work as a separate world that attracts and demands our complete engagement. The challenge of great works to our perceptual, cognitive, and affective capacities, and their full occupation and fulfillment in meeting that challenge, removes us entirely from the real world of our practical affairs. It is in the ultimately satisfying exercise of these different mental capacities operating together to appreciate the rich relational properties of artworks that I shall argue the primary value of great works is to be found. This value of providing us alternative worlds to which we must fully attend will also explain many of the subsidiary values rightly ascribed to works of art. It also provides an alternative way to draw the distinction emphasized by some expressivist theories between art and craft.[9] We all sing, dance, and tell stories, and many of us pursue various other crafts. What distinguishes fine works of art is not simply the degree of skill involved in their production. Nor does the distinction lie in the fact that art but not craft expresses emotion, since many works of art do not do so, at least not at all obviously. There is clearly a distinction, however, in the challenges that great works present to our various mental capacities united in their appreciation and in the pleasure or satisfaction derived from meeting those challenges.

It is common to speak of the world of a novel, the fictional world created by taking all its propositions to be (fictionally) true. Such a world, filled out from the explicit descriptions contained in the text, is populated with more or less ordinary people, places, and objects, albeit fictional ones. There is no such world of nonrepresentational works. But there is another sense indicated above in which not only representational works such as paintings and novels but great works of music as well constitute alternative worlds to challenge and engage us.

All musical perception and understanding requires sensation, cognition, and affect or feeling joined indissolubly in grasping the forms constituted simultaneously by melody, harmony, rhythm, tone, color, and volume in relations of contrast, repetition, variation, and so on. Listeners not only sense but must also *feel* passages containing these elements as introductions, the building of tensions, developments, or resolutions in order to understand the music. Cognitive grasp of a musical work's unfolding, overlapping, and nested forms is at the same time affective reaction to passages always heard as related to previous ones and ones possibly to come. Symphonic music may seem a hard case for the claim that art provides alternative worlds, but this total involvement of its listeners, losing their ordinary identities and practical concerns, indicates a sense in which the claim is true and universal to great art. This claim extends specifically to literature too. Imaginative involvement in the fictional world of a novel's characters is only part of our full engagement with literary works. Other facets include pleasure in the sensuous sound and rhythm of the language and attention to formal structures in relations among characters, plot developments, and so on.

Antecedents

I do not claim complete originality for this thesis regarding the primary value of many great works of art. Certainly there have been more than hints of it among the major writings in aesthetics, above all in those of Kant and Dewey. Writers before Kant in the British tradition had pointed to the lack of practical utility to artworks, to our disinterested attitude in perceiving them. It was a major step to take this superficial or immediate uselessness (in this world) as a key to the primary value of art. For Kant this value lay in the harmonious exercise of the faculties of imagination and understanding in free play, without the imposition of concepts or rules that could reveal a fixed purpose to the aesthetic object.[10]

Kant equated judgments of beauty here with judgments of aesthetic value (or evaluation). And when he wrote of the feeling or form of purposiveness in aesthetic objects without genuine purpose, he was using the concept of purpose in a somewhat idiosyncratic or technical way (referring again, in large part, to the absence of rules that could determine the beauty of an object). But he more than suggests that, first, aesthetic value is to be found in the interrelations among elements within artworks that create a kind of internal logic or purpose that enriches the experience of their audiences without being expressible in fixed rules. Second, Kant is explicit that the pleasure of aesthetic experience derives from the full engagement of our mental faculties operating together and finding fulfillment in the forms of aesthetic objects. Whereas the faculties of imagination and understanding are normally concerned with organizing experience under practical or theoretical concepts, here they are exercised for their own sakes on objects that harmonize their operations. This harmony expresses the felt compatibility between cognition and the sensible object that may be lacking when the latter is subsumed under a set of fixed concepts. Although Kant has little to say here about the expressive content of artworks and their engagement of our affective capacities, all this is quite close to the idea that great artworks provide us alternative worlds in which to become fully and satisfyingly engaged.

As for Dewey, writing at a time when formalist and expressivist theories were vying for predominance, he emphasizes instead the holistic character of aesthetic experience. Experience is aesthetic, he argues, when later parts build on earlier and anticipate still later parts, creating an ultimately unified, full, and self-contained experience. On the side of the aesthetic object, he writes of "the interfusion of all properties of the medium" to serve "the whole creature in his unified vitality."[11] And on the side of the subject, he writes, "Perception that occurs for its own sake is full realization of all the elements of our psychological being."[12] At the same time this full absorption dissolves awareness of the self into perfect union with the aesthetic object. Once more these themes will be echoed in my development of the claim that great art creates alternative worlds as objects of complete and fulfilling engagement. I shall therefore have occasion for further reference to the theories of both Kant and Dewey.

Despite these notable antecedents, the claim that great artworks share certain characteristics, as noted above, runs against currently fashionable views in aesthetics. It may seem to contradict also both certain theses I want to defend and recent developments in art itself. A value that spans historical eras and styles might be rejected out of hand by new historicists (who embrace a relativist historicism without its older monothematic Hegelian dialectic) and by those who offer only sociological explanations for aesthetic tastes. At the extreme of such views, "great" works themselves, especially when removed from their historical and social contexts of production and placed in museums, mainly represent attempts to maintain and reinforce elitist class distinctions.[13] Beyond great works embodying bygone eras, their aesthetic values are determined only by contingent, historically relative standards often rejected by more contemporary art itself. Any claim to the contrary runs afoul of a well-entrenched thesis in aesthetics: that there are no rules for producing or recognizing works of great value.

Some of this extreme aesthetic skepticism I reject, and the remainder, the legitimate points, are compatible with the sort of value I attribute to many works in the canons of great art. That appreciation or taste for "high" art derives only from social programming whose function is to solidify elitist separatism is a thesis belied by contemporary sociological fact. For example, there are members of the upper class who wonder and puzzle no less than others at some of what is presented to them as contemporary art, and there are crowds of a half million who come to hear grand opera in Central Park in New York. Speaking for myself, I know that if my tastes were strictly ideological, I would appreciate certain forms of avant-garde music that would place me among the elite in listeners. But for the most part my preferences do not run that way. The point here is that the Marxist thesis that reduces aesthetic value to sociopolitical currency cannot explain the aesthetic disagreement within social classes or the agreement in taste across classes. The account of aesthetic value to be offered in this book allows for a degree of historical relativism in aesthetic judgments, but it resists and hopefully refutes such strict reductionism.

The thesis, first clearly enunciated by Kant, that there are no aesthetic rules or universal principles precludes a description of universally shared values in terms of objective properties of great works themselves. But this thesis does not preclude a description of their value in terms of their common effects on us, which is the sort of account I offer. This account is compatible with the claim that all objectively describable standards are historically and stylistically relative. Nevertheless, the attack of the avant-garde from within art itself on virtually all standards implicit in the canon, and the subsequent absorption of such art into the canon itself, create problems for any contemporary aesthetic theory, which will have to be addressed, however briefly, below.

Reasons for Evaluations

Kant's thesis that the value of artworks cannot be captured in a set of concepts or rules raises a central issue in regard to evaluations of artworks. In Chapter 5 I will address the issue of evaluative principles and the reasons that can support aesthetic judgments. What would aesthetic principles need to be to govern arguments about the merits of works? They would need to link judgments about nonevaluative properties to the ascriptions of evaluative properties described earlier. It is clear first of all, however, that there are no necessary and sufficient conditions of this sort. Ascriptions of value-neutral properties do not entail evaluations. I will deny also two currently trendy philosophical interpretations of this relation. The first is that evaluative aesthetic properties supervene on objective properties of artworks. (That is, there can be no differences in aesthetic properties without differences in objective properties). The second is that objective properties are criteria (noninductive evidence short of entailment) for evaluative properties. If both these interpretations of the relation are false, then the most interesting question becomes whether the presence of certain objective properties in works always counts in one direction only toward evaluation: whether there are good-making and bad-making nonevaluative properties. Does the presence of lines of certain shapes always contribute to gracefulness, for example, and does gracefulness always contribute to the overall goodness of a painting?

That the primary value of a great work derives from the ways many of its properties interact to interrelate its parts and relate it to its tradition, that this value therefore derives only from the whole work or a substantial portion of it, strongly suggests a negative answer to the question just posed. Nothing short of a whole work engaging us completely and fulfillingly will guarantee positive evaluation. Narrower features taken separately that might interact positively and create value in particular works might distract our attention or be out of harmony with other properties in other works. The value-creating characteristics considered earlier—representation, expression, concise or even elegant form—can, if they completely dominate a work and our attention to it, prevent the more encompassing sort of artistic value from being realized. Thus any objective property of a work, when combined in perception with others, can contribute to or detract from the value of that work.

Another and far more obvious reason for the absence of principles with which to support aesthetic evaluation lies in irreconcilable differences in taste. It is an old cliché that what appeals to one person in art will not appeal to another. But if true, this in itself might block principles that would link nonevaluative to evaluative properties of works in the ways indicated. The negative argument here requires us to posit disagreement at every level of sophistication or education in taste and disagreement not just regarding cases recognized as borderline but over the entire spectrum of evaluative judgments. I believe this claim is plausible, however. If we cannot explain away disagreement in aesthetic evaluations as resulting from ignorance or error, then we cannot link objective properties of works to evaluative properties or evaluations via rules or principles.

The theory holding that evaluative principles are absent is also supported by comparisons between aesthetic and moral judgments. I shall claim that both traditional assimilations of these judgments as well as standardly drawn contrasts are mistaken and misleading. The real contrast lies not in the presence of moral principles whose counterparts are lacking in aesthetics but in a different constraint of coherence (to be spelled out) on moral judgments lacking in the aesthetic realm. The lack of principles, the absence of this constraint, and the widespread disagreements in taste in art will leave us with two major issues for discussion. The first is whether there can be reasons truly supportive of aesthetic evaluations in the absence of principles. The second is whether some tastes are better than others.

Critics do provide reasons for their overall evaluations by ascribing evaluative aesthetic properties to works. They talk of their power, grace, and so on. If pressed to defend these ascriptions, they appeal to nonevaluative properties such as harmonic developments in musical pieces or contours and colors in paintings. In doing so they imply that others ought to share their judgments. But why should we be inclined to accept such alleged reasons in these contexts if they are admitted to be of no relevance in other contexts? If alleged reasons for aesthetic evaluations cannot be generalized at all, then they are not reasons, and aesthetic evaluation becomes a matter of pure personal preference. But some generalization is possible, although not in the form of principles that ignore changing artistic contexts and differences in taste. If the link between objective properties of artworks and evaluations is not reductive, conceptual, criterial, or one of supervenience, then it must be simply inductive or causal. In ascribing evaluative aesthetic properties to works and in making overall evaluative judgments, critics are implying that those with developed tastes similar to their own will react to the same objective properties of the works in the same ways. This may not seem to be saying much, but it serves several functions for audiences and potential audiences.

First, those who want information about what in the art world might interest them tend to find critics who generally share their tastes. Given common tastes, they ought to agree in the ascription of evaluative properties such as power or elegance when they come to see the objective properties on which these ascriptions are based. Second, as noted above, critics not only ascribe evaluative aesthetic properties but also indicate those objective properties of works to which they are reacting in making such ascriptions. By doing so they may suggest new interpretations of works—new ways of understanding potential aesthetic values in the works' properties— even for those who do not generally share the critics' tastes. Any plausible way of linking value-neutral properties to evaluative aesthetic properties can be a guide to the perceptions of those viewing the work, especially those who want to develop or educate their tastes in works of that kind.

Taste

To relativize evaluations to different tastes and leave it at that would be to imply that a typical 1950s rock song is as good as *The Marriage of Figaro* and that pulp romances are as good as *Middle-*

march. To avoid this implication, we therefore relativize judgments only to those with developed or educated tastes. But this raises the final question for discussion in the last chapter: In what sense are developed tastes better? or, more generally, What grounds do we have for claiming that some tastes are better than others? Here we must first distinguish better from worse taste, and this can be done by pointing to distinguishing features of their respective objects of approval. Then we must indicate why we ought to prefer to have the sort of taste deemed better according to these criteria. This will at the same time provide a rationale for educational programs that aim to educate taste in art.

Many rationales typically offered by art educators are problematic or unsupported. Claims that aesthetic perception of the "higher" sort promotes general cognitive development (better than studying, say, logic?), trains us to experience in general more perceptively, or develops our affective and moral capacities so that we relate to other persons better fall into the class of the empirically unsupported. A more promising approach might appeal simply to the great pleasures derived from appreciating fine art. But there are problems here, too, if the proposal is that fine art offers greater pleasure than more popular forms of culture or entertainment. Those forms have their fanatical devotees in larger numbers. Nor, absent the sort of education or indoctrination that is in question, do those who have experienced both higher- and lower-brow culture often prefer the former.

If we are to speak of pleasure in this context, then we had better follow Mill in distinguishing not quantity but quality of pleasure afforded by different objects to different tastes. Better taste must offer the prospect not of more pleasure but of a deeper or ultimately fuller satisfaction. This claim is partially supported by our inclination to think of worse taste as shallow or superficial. But I prefer to cash out these metaphors by referring directly once again to the challenge of great art to combine our mental capacities in fulfilling ways. Meeting this challenge results in a multidimensional experience richer than that derivable from simpler objects and pursuits.

Although even fully educated and developed tastes can and do differ, there is a natural quest for consensus in aesthetic judgments. The feeling of unity with others who share taste in cultural matters can be a powerful social force, as Marxist aestheticians point out (often with censorious intent). This feeling may be stronger because consensus is arrived at freely, not under constraint of rules or prin-

What are the source of aesthetic value?

ciples. Cultural agreement is similar to moral agreement in building a sense of community according to common values. Artworks as other worlds can imply criticism of experience in the real world, can project possibilities for richer experience outside art, or simply offer an escape from everyday experience. Experiencing such worlds in common creates social bonds that reinforce bonds from other cooperative activities. The desire to share these rich experiences, and the impetus to seek that consensus in aesthetic judgment that prompts and expresses such sharing, is another explanation for the primacy of evaluation and reference to values in discourse about art. A philosophical account that explains the general grounds for such potentially shared values can contribute to the quest for mutual aesthetic appreciation. I hope to provide such an account in subsequent chapters.

complex

artwork are, other worlds
with rich relational objective properties
that challenge/engage us

art experience — different mental capacities operating together — total involvement — full engagement

aesthetic judgments are evaluative judgments rest on ascribing aesthetic properties to art works

gives most art true but enhanced of values appreciation

aesthetic judgments (are evaluative)
terms
↓
ascribe
aesthetic properties (evaluative)

CHAPTER TWO

Evaluative Aesthetic Properties

base properties

Classification and Nature

Artworks are rarely conceived or described as mere physical objects or processes. Critics and laypersons alike invariably ascribe properties to them beyond those described in purely physical terms. They use a large variety of terms in ascribing these properties. First, there are broadly evaluative terms: beautiful, ugly, sublime, dreary; second, formal terms: balanced, graceful, concise, loosely woven; third, emotion terms: sad, angry, joyful, serene; fourth, evocative terms: powerful, stirring, amusing, hilarious, boring; fifth, behavioral terms: sluggish, bouncy, jaunty; sixth, representational terms: realistic, distorted, true to life, erroneous; seventh, second-order perceptual terms: vivid, dull, muted, steely, mellow (ascribed to colors or tones); eighth, historical terms: derivative, original, daring, bold, conservative.

This chapter will be concerned with the nature of the properties picked out by these terms. If they are typical terms of art criticism and evaluation, then understanding the nature of these properties will give us a good start toward understanding the bases for aesthetic evaluation and the sources of aesthetic value. Are these properties, for example, special kinds of qualities in art objects themselves, or do these terms refer to our subjective reactions to more ordinary kinds of properties in the objects themselves? If the latter, to what sorts of properties are we typically reacting, and why are they sources of aesthetic value? This chapter will answer the first of these questions, and the next chapter will answer the second.

17

Many of these terms have been said to ascribe aesthetic properties to artworks, and we might as well extend this class to include all
the aforementioned terms and the properties they pick out. But a
common label is misleading unless there is some other common feature that these properties share. None, we have noted, is a merely
physical property. All seem to encompass some way in which we
experience or react to the physical properties of artworks. It might
be suggested that aesthetic properties are phenomenal properties of
artworks, characterizing ways we perceive them. Some considerations support this suggestion. First, when told to attend aesthetically to some object, most of us would take this to mean that we are
to attend to its appearance, to its phenomenal or perceivable properties, and to abstract from other relations it bears to us and to
other objects. Second, when we ascribe emotion properties to a
piece of music, for example, we do not mean *only* that the music
arouses corresponding emotions in us (whether we mean that at all
will be discussed in the next chapter). We must also perceive those
emotion properties (perhaps only metaphorically) in the work itself.

Nevertheless, we must admit also that not all the above-men-
tioned terms refer to properties entirely perceivable in artworks
themselves. First, even those that do so refer require knowledge of
contexts and causal factors external to the works in order to be correctly applied. Which emotion qualities a work expresses, for example, may well depend on the style in which it is composed or
painted and on the expressive resources available to composers or
artists working in that style. Expressive qualities can differ from an
original painting to an exact copy, although all the perceivable qualities are the same. The expressiveness derived from the anguished
brush strokes of a Van Gogh, for example, may be absent in a copy
for the knowledgeable viewer, since the brush strokes in the copy
no longer reflect its producer's anguish. Second, many of the properties indicated above are not perceivable at all in works themselves.
Even formal qualities that normally are directly perceivable may
not be in a long novel or complex musical piece. And other of these
properties consist in relations between artworks or their intrinsic
qualities and phenomena outside them. Being true to life is a relation between a work and its model or referent; being original or
daring is a relation of a work to its tradition.

Another suggestion is that aesthetic qualities are regional properties, qualities of complex objects that emerge from properties of their parts.[1] Many of the properties mentioned do arise from complex relations among simpler parts and from simpler formal relations among elements within works. This is one reason why those not trained or experienced in viewing artworks often do not see their aesthetic properties as readily as they see their simpler perceptual properties. But again the generalization is not always true. Vividness of color and mellowness or steeliness of tone are immediately perceptible, and simple objects can be beautiful, amusing, dreary, or distorted.

Perhaps the most famous suggestion in this area was the first systematic attempt to classify these properties: Frank Sibley's claim that aesthetic properties are those that require taste to be perceived.[2] Once more the plausibility of this claim derives first from the fact that naive perceivers do not see serenity, grace, or power in artworks as readily as they see redness and squareness. 'Taste' refers partly (when not preceded by 'bad') to the sophistication of trained viewers who can immediately perceive the aesthetic properties of works, even when these properties consist in complex relations. It also refers to the evaluative component in aesthetic judgment, to the fact that ascribing many of these qualities to a work implies some judgment of its worth. To call a work sublime, concise, stirring, or bold is to express a positive judgment; to call it dreary, derivative, sluggish, or boring is to judge negatively. The appeal to taste indicates the subjective variability of these judgments as well. What is concise to one critic is truncated to another; what is stirring or vivid to one is strident or garish to another.

Nevertheless, despite the fact that taste in these various senses is involved in ascribing many of these properties, the ascription of others fails to involve taste (in one or more sense). To call a piece of music sad, for example, is not necessarily to evaluate it. Vividness in color or steeliness in the tone of a trumpet is neither directly evaluative nor a complex relation that requires training to be perceived. Thus, if these are included among aesthetic qualities, as I believe they should and intuitively would be, then not all such properties can be characterized as those that require taste to be perceived. Furthermore, to speak, as Sibley does, of *requiring* taste, or of properties being perceived by means of taste, strongly suggests the

eighteenth-century concept of a special faculty akin to moral intu-
ition. But in both cases there is no suggestion of how such a faculty
might work, nor indeed any evidence of its existence. We must seek
a different way of characterizing aesthetic properties if indeed they
do constitute a distinct class.

I have said that not all the terms in our list are used to express
evaluations. Not all the properties they name consist in relations
that include evaluative responses. But those that are not evaluative,
for example, emotion properties such as sadness, nevertheless are
of a type that ground other evaluative properties (for example,
poignancy) and hence evaluations. Thus we may characterize aesthetic properties as those that contribute to the aesthetic values of
artworks (or in some cases to the aesthetic values of natural objects
or scenes). In offering this characterization we must remember that
some of these values are negative, making works worse. If being
dreary, derivative, dull, or sluggish contributes to a work's value,
the contribution is normally only to the work's negative value. We
must also not imagine, even for the positively evaluative properties
(those that normally include relations to positively evaluative responses), that the more artists build such properties into their
works, the better their works will be. Creating a great work is not
so simple, since many of these properties will counteract the normally positive effects of others in the wrong contexts.

Despite these qualifications, we may accept as our basic criterion
for identifying aesthetic properties that they are those that ground
or instantiate in their relations to us or other properties those values
of artworks that make them worth contemplating. If we accept an
evaluative concept of art according to which artworks are artifacts
that reward sustained contemplation, then aesthetic properties are
also those that determine artifacts to be works of art (second criterion) and that determine what kinds of artworks they are.[3] I do not
want to claim, however, that this is the exclusively correct definition of 'artwork'. I also do not want to claim that aesthetic properties can always be clearly distinguished from others, that there are
no borderline cases. There will be borderline cases in this area when
knowledgeable critics disagree in evaluations and hence possibly
disagree about which properties ground or instantiate aesthetic
value. But borderline cases do not in themselves destroy the useful-
ness of distinctions.

As a third criterion we might view aesthetic properties as those
that critics need to point out and justify ascribing. This criterion is

subsidiary, since it is explained by our first one. Because critics aim at showing the values of artworks and evaluating them, because they offer interpretations aimed at maximizing those values for their readers, and because aesthetic properties are those that ground or instantiate those values, critics are most concerned with the aesthetic properties of artworks. Normally, they will justify ascriptions of the more broadly evaluative of these properties by appeal to the less broadly evaluative. We may now begin to show how this process of justification works by first analyzing more closely the typical structure of these properties.

The Humean Structure

I have said that many of the terms on our list are used to express approval or disapproval as well as to indicate objective properties of the works to which they apply. Those that do not themselves express evaluative reactions nevertheless express reactions, ways of perceiving or feeling, that help to ground evaluations or evaluative responses. At the same time, ascribing the properties named by these terms as if they were simply objective properties of works strongly suggests that other viewers ought to share the judgments asserted. These expressive and normative aspects of aesthetic judgments (those that ascribe aesthetic properties) are essential to their being the kind of judgment they are.

All three functions of aesthetic judgments—objective (or assertive), expressive, and normative—are captured by an analysis of a form that might be used to characterize secondary qualities (such as colors) and moral properties (such as rightness) as well. The form may be schematized as follows:

Object O has aesthetic property P = O is such as to elicit response of kind R in ideal viewers of kind V in virtue of its more basic properties B.

For the aesthetic properties on our list, V will remain relatively constant, but R and B will vary depending on the type of property P is.

Reference to the constant properties V of ideal viewers captures the normative side of judgments ascribing aesthetic properties. V will include being knowledgeable, unbiased, sensitive, and of developed taste (if this involves more than knowledge and sensitivity).

That critics with these characteristics would react positively to a work suggests that others ought to as well. This may be because, as I shall argue in a later chapter, such critics derive deeper enjoyments from aesthetic appreciation. But whether or not this case can be made, ordinary viewers would like to think of themselves as sensitive and knowledgeable or at least as making judgments shared by critics with those qualities. They will normally agree with what they conceive as an ideal judgment. This is not a matter of entailment, since viewers can sometimes recognize artistic merit in works to which they are not personally attracted. But then, although they might stick to their personal responses as bases for their overall evaluative judgments, it would be more normal in this situation for them to judge positively, in accordance with their conception of judgments of those more sensitive, despite their personal reactions.

The knowledge that ideal critics must have includes not only knowledge of the type of work to which O belongs but also of contrasting works and of the historical (social, cultural) milieu in which the work fits. By 'unbiased', I do not mean to rule out preferences in taste or social point of view, only such obvious disqualifications as personal relation to the artist. The reference to sensitivity among the qualities defining V may be problematic in introducing circularity into the analysis. If being sensitive is being able to appreciate aesthetic properties and the values to which they contribute, and an aesthetic property is one that causes a certain kind of response in a sensitive viewer, then we do have a problem of circularity. One way of removing it would be by adopting a weak notion of sensitivity as powers of sensory discrimination. If critics cannot discriminate the relevant properties of contrasted works, they certainly cannot judge which are better. Another way to avoid circularity would be by appeal to paradigms, works to which any ideal (sensitive) critic must react positively. Perhaps we would not require of ideal critics positive reactions to all paradigms, but a sensitive critic would need to give reasons for a negative evaluation of any such work.

The response to which R in the schema refers indicates the expressive aspect of aesthetic judgments. It will vary first according to whether P is an evaluative property. If it is, then R will be positive or negative, often involving pleasure or displeasure. Although the evocative qualities named above most obviously include in their relations reactions of observers, the Humean account analyzes other aesthetic properties as having the same structure. All are relations that include responses of ideal viewers or critics, at least until we arrive at base properties, which are relations wholly within works or between works and other objects. Such properties, if basic for aesthetic judgments, ultimately ground the responses of ideal critics.

Aesthetic properties may be more or less strongly evaluative and more or less specific on their objective sides. Ascriptions of more strongly evaluative and less objectively specific properties must be justified by appeal to less purely evaluative and more objectively specific properties. Such ascriptions imply that ideal critics respond in virtue of or because of the latter properties, that their responses are not to aesthetically irrelevant grounds. This process of justification will continue under challenge until it arrives at objective relations, often formal relations, that ultimately ground evaluative responses.

Beauty, for example, is unspecific on the objective side but always elicits a pleasurable response from sensitive observers. It is unspecific in that its ascription leaves unspecified how the object is such as to elicit this positive response in suitable viewers. An artwork may be beautiful by virtue of its grace or balance or power or vivid colors. It may in turn be graceful by virtue of its delicate lines, balanced by virtue of its symmetrical composition, powerful because of its piercing poignancy, vivid because of its highly saturated colors. Finally, its lines may be delicate because of their thin, smooth curves, and its poignancy may derive from its subtle expression of deep sadness (perhaps to be further specified in terms of formal causes). To be discussed below in this chapter and the next are the nature of these dependence relations and the nature of the base, nonevaluative properties, the reasons why they can ground evaluative properties, and why they are sources of value.

In regard to beauty, philosophers have not always agreed that its objective side cannot be specified. Perhaps the most famous attempt to do so was that of Francis Hutcheson, who held that it is always uniformity amid variety that elicits aesthetic pleasure expressed in ascriptions of beauty.[4] One possibility here is that 'uniformity' and 'variety' are themselves used evaluatively, beginning a chain of justification such as those described above, which could end in an indefinite and various collection of objective properties. In that case Hutcheson has failed to specify an objective base for beauty. The other possibility is that these concepts are not themselves evaluative. But then it is easy to imagine complex artworks and other objects that also have some unifying qualities—say a single drab, brown color and squat, sharply jutting lines—that are not at all beautiful. Either way the attempt at objective specification fails.

Attempts continue to be made on occasion, but contemporary accounts fare no better. For Guy Sircello, to take one, beauty consists in having certain other properties to a high degree. Properties that admit of qualitative degrees relative to objects that have them are beautiful when possessed to a high degree, according to his theory of beauty.[5] His paradigm is vividness in colors. But, aside from the fact that the theory emphasizes sensuous beauty at the expense of formal beauty (emphasized by Hutcheson), it fails even in its paradigm case. On the one hand, a pastel may be beautiful without our being tempted to say that it is a vivid pastel (if that would be coherent). On the other hand, a color that is beautifully vivid to one observer may be simply garish to another, not in the sense that its beauty is overridden or defeated by its garishness but in that it is simply garish instead of beautiful. Likewise, the same color that is beautiful in the context of one color scheme may be offensive in the context of another. In the latter context, there is no reason to say that it remains beautiful in itself; rather, beauty of color, like perception of color, seems to be in part a function of context. If this theory therefore fails in its paradigm case, then there is no need to press the more obvious objection that qualities like sliminess become more rather than less distasteful the greater the degree to which they are present.

The final attempt at the specification of the objective side of beauty that we can consider consists in the claim, made since antiquity, that certain configurations of tones and certain shapes (for example, circles and particular rectangles) are intrinsically pleasing or beautiful to us. If this were so, it would have no more interest than the fact that certain flowers and sunsets are deemed beautiful by almost all viewers. The claim does not begin to provide a full specification or theory of beauty. The further problem here is that the same objection in regard to context can be made as in the case of colors that may when isolated strike many or most as beautiful. Circles too may constitute beautiful forms in one context but be merely offensive in others (as the shape of a human body, for example).

Thus ascriptions of beauty and other purely evaluative properties require chains of justification that may differ in their middle and base levels. But as we move down these chains, the evaluative properties mentioned will become more specific on their objective sides. 'Graceful' always refers to formal properties, and only of certain kinds. Thick, straight, and sharply angular lines rarely make for a graceful drawing, and squat objects with jutting edges cannot be graceful. A graceful sculpture ordinarily has smooth and flowing curves and lacks sharply protruding parts. (This is not to say that smooth curves always tend to make an object graceful. Such stronger claims will be examined later.) A daring or innovative work must contain features not possessed by its predecessors in the tradition to which it is related, features of which ideal critics approve (the latter explaining why not all works with novel features are innovative or daring). In the cases of both grace and innovation, the objective properties that elicit approval, which are partially but not completely indicated by the ascriptions of the evaluative properties, themselves consist in relations, in the one case formal and in the other historical. This is typical of these middle-level evaluative aesthetic properties.

Ultimately a critic or viewer should defend evaluations by indicating nonevaluative properties of the works being judged. These base-level reasons for aesthetic judgments will be formal, expressive, representational, symbolic, or historical properties (relations to a tradition) of the work that lack evaluative dimensions in themselves. We can illustrate the difference between properties that are evaluative in themselves and those that merely ground evaluations by further examples. To say that a painting's composition is balanced may be to evaluate it positively; to say that it is symmetrical is not evaluative. To say that a musical composition is poignant expresses a positive reaction; to call it sad does not. To describe a novel's structure or forms of expression as bold and innovative suggests approval; to call them new or never experienced before is evaluatively neutral. When justifying ascription of an evaluative property, final appeal may be always to nonevaluative formal properties, but this claim is more controversial.

The fact-value distinction drawn here is (I hope) not naive, insofar as one thrust of the previous discussion is that many terms of aesthetic discourse and properties to which they refer cut across this distinction. Ascriptions of almost all but the base properties are both evaluative (expressive and normative) and descriptive. But the fact that, according to our Humean analysis, evaluative responses of ideal critics are always based on properties of artworks they confront implies that ultimately there must be nonevaluative properties on which their judgments are based. Such properties may be, and typically are, relational, but they are not relations to evaluative responses of subjects.

A different question is whether we can always analyze evaluative properties into evaluative and nonevaluative components. Since we have viewed these properties as relations between objective properties and evaluative responses, it might seem that the answer must be affirmative. But I have also pointed out that many of the higher-level properties of this sort are unspecific on their objective sides. Although it should be possible in principle to analyze specific references to such properties into objective and subjective components, we cannot do so for the properties themselves. And we may not be able to eliminate the "in principle" qualifier even in the case of specific references, since we may lack other terms to describe the particular subjective feel expressed by use of the term in question. This is not troubling, however, since the task of justifying aesthetic judgments requires only being able to specify their objective bases in the contexts in which they are made.

Finally, I do not mean to suggest by noting that ascriptions of higher-level evaluative properties must be based on lower-level (and ultimately on nonevaluative) properties that we typically first perceive the base properties. We can first notice the attitude of calm resignation in the painting of Whistler's mother by perceiving its subdued mood and perhaps without yet consciously noting its muted colors, soft lines, and subtle balance. It is the latter to which we are responding affectively and to which we would ultimately appeal in defending an evaluation of the painting. But we may notice these properties only when challenged to justify our more immediate but higher-level descriptions. At the same time, those who do not respond affectively to the painting, who do not yet see its forceful yet tranquil quality, can be brought to do so by critics or teachers who begin by pointing out the objective properties to which their students are to respond.

Realism

The heading of this section refers to philosophical realism about aesthetic properties generally, not to naturalistic representation (which will be discussed briefly later). A property is real in the relevant sense if the truth of its ascription is independent of the subject's evidence and system of beliefs. It is possible for one to make an error about the presence of a real property despite its appearing to be present and despite one's belief in its presence cohering with other beliefs. If aesthetic qualities are real properties of objects, then there must be some distinction possible between how they appear and how they are. Reality is always conceivably distinct from appearance and from the way it is believed to be.

It may seem that, according to the analysis offered above, aesthetic properties cannot be real in this sense. Since responses of subjects (usually evaluative responses) are partly constitutive of these relational properties, it may seem that they are simply ways certain objects appear to subjects with aesthetic sensibilities. Then the crucial distinction between the ways aesthetic properties of objects appear to evaluating subjects and the ways they really are seems to vanish. But in fact the analysis does not in itself defeat realism with regard to aesthetic properties. Surprisingly, it is its reference to ideal rather than actual viewers that can be held to support a realist position. These ideal viewers or critics are those to whom aesthetic properties appear as they are. The judgments of others will then reflect mere appearances to the extent that they differ from judgments of ideal critics. Furthermore, real judgments can be mistaken however much they cohere with others that reflect the tastes or experiences of fallible or nonideal critics. Thus the distinctions required by the realist can be drawn here.

As noted briefly above, the analysis of aesthetic properties is similar in structure to a plausible account of colors and other secondary qualities. There again the way an object appears in ideal conditions to normal perceivers is held to be constitutive of the color it has; judgments that differ from those of such perceivers in such conditions reflect only apparent colors. Colors themselves are thought of as relations between physical properties of objects (configurations of molecules on their surfaces that determine how they reflect light) and perceptual responses of normal perceivers. Despite being relations to these responses, they are real in the requisite sense in allowing for mere appearance and error. At least they will be real if normal perceivers can be specified in a noncircular way and if those perceivers agree in their judgments of colors.[6] Similarly, the issue for aesthetic properties, conceived as higher-order relations involving responses to (formal relations among) such perceptual properties as colors and tones, is whether the realist can specify a class of ideal perceivers or critics to whom these properties appear as they are.

If such specification is possible, then real aesthetic properties can also explain the aesthetic judgments of actual critics, insofar as they approximate to the knowledge and other features of ideal critics and judge as they do because they have these features. Aesthetic knowledge is knowledge of what would elicit the responses of ideal critics, of the objective bases for ideal evaluations. This knowledge can be used to criticize actual evaluative judgments when these are explained by deviations of real critics from characteristics of ideal ones. If real audiences are inattentive, uneducated, biased (influenced by irrelevant personal associations), or insensitive, then they can miss the grace, power, or beauty of an artwork. They will react in the wrong way or to the wrong properties. Thus, in appreciating these properties, they do not express merely their own reactions but also their belief or knowledge that critics who share none of these defects would react and judge in the same ways when confronted by the same works or properties.

Finally, real aesthetic properties as so characterized could explain and predict not only the ways critics will respond to works but also the ways artists will produce them, given their preferences and tastes. This critic does not appreciate subtle grace; therefore he will not like this painting. That artist paints as she does to create dynamic tension in her compositions. The realist posits real aesthetic properties precisely to be able to offer such explanations, because of the explanatory value of appealing to these properties. According to him, nonrealists cannot offer explanations of this sort. Aesthetic properties cannot explain responses expressed in aesthetic judgments if appeal to them refers only to those responses themselves. If we are to believe in those properties to which our best explanatory theories must refer, then according to the realist we ought to believe in real aesthetic properties.

Whether the realist's claim is correct and whether the nonrealist can offer comparable explanations remain to be seen. The prior issue is whether ideal critics as specified above in terms of their characteristics (V) will agree in their aesthetic judgments. The account can qualify as realist because, despite the subjective sides of these relational properties, the responses of ideal viewers and the properties that elicit them remain independent of the beliefs of actual viewers about these relations. But if ideal critics disagree in their aesthetic judgments, then the account will have us ascribing incompatible properties to the same artworks. Works will be both graceful and not graceful, powerful and not powerful. The issue of agreement among ideal critics is crucial, since the account becomes incoherent without such consensus.

It should now be clear why realists emphasize agreements in judgments ascribing aesthetic properties whereas nonrealists emphasize disagreements or differences in taste. It is not that agreement or disagreement in itself implies their positions. Whether real viewers agree in their aesthetic judgments is on this account merely evidence for the pattern of judgments among ideal critics. Put another way, it is the best explanation for actual agreements or disagreements that is crucial for the issue of realism. If agreement is the norm and disagreements can be explained by appeal to the ways disputants deviate from characteristics or conditions of ideal audiences, then realism can be maintained. Thus, for realists the explanation why virtually every music lover agrees that the opening phrases of Mozart's Fortieth Symphony and Beethoven's Sixth Symphony are beautiful is that these opening bars *are* beautiful and that experienced listeners can perceive their beauty. There is a property of beauty independent of judgments ascribing it that grounds and explains those judgments. On our account, that property is constituted by the same objective properties of the work eliciting the same responses from ideal critics. Those who disagree here simply do not perceive this property (or, more precisely, do not react to the objective properties of these works as ideal critics do) because they are inattentive, insensitive, lack knowledge, and so on—that is, because of the ways they deviate from ideal critics.

Antirealists, by contrast, will emphasize disagreements in more controversial cases. One critic finds Tchaikovsky's Sixth Symphony powerfully poignant and another finds it self-indulgently maudlin. One concertgoer believes Saint-Saëns to be a first-rate composer and better than Vivaldi; another disagrees. For nonrealists there are no facts of the matter here. The disagreements are not to be explained by ignorance, bias, or insensitivity. If not, then the realist relational account once more will ascribe incompatible properties to these works and artists. Of course, the nonrealist must also explain the agreements to which the realist points. Nonrealists will explain the agreements on Mozart's Fortieth and Beethoven's Sixth symphonies in terms of common musical tastes or sensibilities de-

veloped from similar training or musical upbringing without appealing to an independent property of beauty perceived in these
cases. Listeners with common cultural backgrounds will react in
similar ways to the sensual and formal properties of these symphonies, but a real property of beauty would be perceived with far
more regularity than we find in ascriptions of this property.

Once more it does not follow from that fact that actual evaluators disagree that ideal critics would do so as well. But if the disagreements among actual evaluators cannot be explained by the
ways in which they deviate from ideal ones, then it would seem that
these disputes would extend into the ideal class as well. Perhaps the
stipulation of additional properties for ideal critics (and hence further ways in which actual audiences might differ from them) would
extend the possibilities for such explanation by realists. But they
might face a dilemma here. On the one hand, if features of ideal
critics are very remote from those of real ones, including sensitivities to differences that we cannot even discriminate, then disagreement among those who satisfy such conditions *might* disappear.
But then we would have no way of judging how they would ascribe
aesthetic properties in concrete presently controversial cases. Thus
this answer to the nonrealist lands us in skepticism regarding
knowledge of these properties (the most common threat to all
forms of realism). This tack would also make it less likely that appeal to such critics could be included in a plausible analysis of what
we mean by ascribing such properties. On the other hand, if we assign features to ideal evaluators that might be approximated by real
ones (as we did), then we have good evidence that disagreements
will persist. We return to the problem of incoherence for the realist.

The realist might attempt to reduce the number of apparent disagreements among ideal critics by trying to show that some apparently ideal critics do not really qualify or, alternatively, by relativizing their definitions to particular art forms and perhaps even styles
within them. We may consider these strategies in relation to classical music lovers versus rock music lovers. The first strategy would
claim that the former are superior judges of music on the ground
that we can explain the latter's low opinion of classical music by appeal to their lack of training, exposure, or sensitivity. Taking rock
music lovers to be ideal critics would leave unexplained the illusion
of beauty or greatness suffered by those who take every opportunity to listen to Mozart or Beethoven. The idea again is to single

out the class of ideal listeners in terms of the overall best explanatory theory.

The initial but not insuperable problem here is that the claimed asymmetry in explanatory power could be challenged. The rock lovers might similarly seek to explain the classicist's taste by appeal to their effete overintellectualizing, social pretension, and educational brainwashing, which they feel result in a loss of sensitivity to basic, driving rhythm and pure harmonic and melodic forms. (My son has so argued in seeking control of our car radio.) The problem can be overcome only if we can show that the taste for classical music is better. This could be done only by compiling a set of agreed good pieces in each genre and finding common characteristics that could be shown to be more often characteristics of classical pieces. I leave this task for later chapters but express my initial optimism here of being able to complete it.

The greater difficulty is the plausibility of the nonrealist's claim that disagreement would persist in the ascription of aesthetic properties to classical pieces by ideal classical music lovers. Such disagreement survives extensive training in musical theory. This takes us to the second strategy mentioned above: Some remaining disputes could be eliminated or resolved by allowing as ideal only critics sensitive to the virtues of pieces in particular styles. Then ideal critics of baroque music would differ from those for romantic music; critics for quartets might differ from those for symphonies; and so on. The problem here is that the outcome of this process of narrowing criteria might be to endorse positive evaluations whenever one educated critic could be found to approve of a work. Why would that critic not be seen as more sensitive to the presence of a real aesthetic property than others? But then the criterion for ascribing such properties (when they are positively evaluative) becomes far too lenient.

At a certain point in this process, however, realists might claim that there was sufficient agreement on central cases to ground the ascription of real aesthetic properties. They could then hold remaining disagreement to indicate only normal vagueness in our concepts of these properties or indeterminacy in the boundary areas between the properties. Eddy Zemach has recently defended aesthetic realism by arguing that there must be such core agreement in the use of aesthetic terms.[7] His paradigm case argument rests on the fact that at least most aesthetic properties are observable. We can learn the meanings of observation terms, he points out, only by learning the objects and properties to which they correctly apply. We, or at least standard observers, must agree in these paradigm applications if our observation terms are to be commonly comprehensible. Without such agreement in the use of aesthetic terms, therefore, there could be no aesthetic judgments in which ideal critics could disagree. Their terms must share a common core of reference for genuine disagreements to arise, since such disputes presuppose common meanings for the terms whose applications to particular cases are in dispute. This core, necessary for aesthetic terms to have stable meanings, suffices to ground reference to real properties, although there naturally remains disagreement on borderline cases. If the core agreement is both necessary for common meaning and sufficient to allow the realist's account of aesthetic properties, then the antirealist's position is incoherent.

But is agreement on paradigms sufficient to ground reference to real aesthetic properties? The nonrealist must acknowledge that nearly all music lovers will agree that Mozart and Beethoven wrote beautiful and powerful music. But it still must be the case that disagreement results from faults in some of the critics or from vagueness at the boundaries of the terms' applications (which afflicts most predicates and perhaps properties as well). These two factors do not seem to exhaust the causes of aesthetic dispute, however. First, unlike the case of secondary qualities such as colors, we cannot unproblematically say that those who disagree with standard judgments about aesthetic qualities are not standard or even ideal critics. Unlike the situation of color-blind perceivers, in many cases here we cannot find defects, independently of their deviant judgments, in art critics who confidently make such judgments and oppose them to the majority views. There are, for example, no specifiable physical defects that underlie their deviance. Whereas many music listeners who avoid Beethoven or Mahler may lack sensitivity to any of the great composers, there are others who are musically well educated and otherwise fully sensitive to the subtleties of complex compositions. Hence there is no explanation from the realist's perspective for their failure to perceive those real aesthetic properties that other trained critics perceive.

Second, not all cases in which we find substantial disagreement without explicable error or defect clearly fall in the borderline areas between correct and incorrect application of their aesthetic terms.

The situation is very different from ordinary cases of vagueness, as with red and orange or bald and hairy. In the area of aesthetic judgment, what one critic finds clearly powerful another finds merely raucous or strident. What one finds deeply poignant, indeed a paradigm and not a borderline instance of poignancy, another finds overwhelmingly self-indulgent or sentimental. This lack of agreement as to where the borders lie prevents our relegating all persistent disagreement in ascriptions of aesthetic properties to the gray areas between the properties and their neighbors. To do so would render too many confident judgments of educated critics about alleged clear-cut instantiations simply incorrect, without any explanation for why such mistakes should be made. In regard to our previous examples, perhaps Saint-Saëns and Vivaldi lie on the borderline of greatness for composers, where disagreement is to be expected. But Tchaikovsky's Sixth is either poignant or maudlin (if these properties are real)—there seems to be no gray area between these.

The more direct response to Zemach's argument is that agreement on paradigms is not necessary for grounding the meanings of aesthetic terms so that parties to aesthetic disputes can comprehend one another. The fact is that disagreements in the applications of these terms are limited in ways sufficient to allow for common meanings but insufficient to make a claim of reference to real properties plausible. What one critic finds gaudy another will not find subtle or bland but may find bold and striking. What impresses one as sprightly and delicate will not impress another as heavy and plodding but might be perceived as flippant and slightly insipid or lacking in substance. These examples suggest that the critics agree in their perceptions of the objective (nonevaluative), formal properties of the works in question but disagree in their evaluative responses to those properties.

This last claim can be made despite my previous admission that we cannot specify analyses of aesthetic properties themselves into evaluative and nonevaluative components. These components will vary with occasions and contexts for ascriptions of these properties, but we can see by the sorts of disagreements we find (and do not find) that the focus of most educated dispute lies on the evaluative side. Being gaudy and being vivid and bold may involve identical objective constituent properties, and that is why these properties can be the focus of critical disagreements. Grounding to common objective components will suffice to make aesthetic property terms comprehensible. This is so even in the absence of shared paradigms to which they are applied if the evaluative uses of these terms can be identified in some way other than by appeal to shared paradigms. And indeed, we can easily identify evaluative import or response by functional role, essentially the expression of approval or disapproval.[8] We have seen that the expressive function, as opposed to reference to the objective (nonevaluative), formal component, will be more or less paramount depending on the particular aesthetic term being used. Together, these factors render usage sufficiently regular for shared meanings and genuine disagreements. Then, too, many of these terms are learned and used outside aesthetic contexts, where there may be greater agreement in their use. It may be natural to extend their use to aesthetic contexts without the same agreement (or possibility of learning the terms originally) there.[9] In short, meaning does not require agreement on core cases of application of aesthetic terms to artworks, and the realist's argument fails.

Zemach offers a second argument to the effect that scientific realists must be realists about aesthetic properties as well.[10] Scientific realists believe in those entities and properties that are posited by theories that provide overall best explanations. (They believe that the truth of these theories, which presuppose such entities and properties, is independent of evidence for them.) But, argues Zemach, the criteria according to which theories are judged explanatorily best are mainly aesthetic. They involve such factors as simplicity, elegance, coherence or unity, and so on. These are among the formal properties to which we appeal when evaluating the forms of artworks; they are aesthetic properties. Hence, scientists have no sound reason to believe their theories true (or that the entities and properties posited by them exist) unless these theories really have the aesthetic properties they believe them to have. If they only appear to have these properties, or if such properties appear only relative to varying tastes, then the reason for believing in explanatorily best theories collapses.

Although Zemach does not do so, we can extend the scope of this argument to appeal not only to realists about the theoretical entities of science but also to realists about ordinary physical objects (whose realism is far less controversial). We can extend the scope in this way if, as I have argued elsewhere, our ultimate justification for believing in the reality of physical objects (although not the normal cause of our believing in them) is that appeal to them best explains ways things appear to us.[11] Here too explanatory virtue is our criterion of reality, and if this virtue is mainly aesthetic, then aesthetic realism would seem to have priority epistemologically (although not commonsensically) over other forms.

The argument is nevertheless limited in scope in a different way. If sound, it directly justifies us in believing only a small subclass of aesthetic properties real, in fact only a small subset of the formal aesthetic properties, which make up only one of many different kinds. Perhaps establishing realism for some aesthetic properties goes a long way toward establishing it for all. But in critically evaluating this argument, it is interesting to note first that only those formal properties that might independently seem more objective (than, say, the expressive properties of artworks) enter into evaluations of scientific theories. Such properties include simplicity and coherence.

Second, we must ask whether such properties as simplicity are the same when ascribed to scientific theories and artworks. Our suspicion that these properties may be only roughly analogous may be aroused by recognizing that the term 'simple' does not have the same evaluative import in art criticism as in science. Whereas what is called simplicity in scientific theories is always, other things equal, a theoretical virtue, simplicity in artistic design, even if equated with unity or coherence, does not always tend to make artworks better (despite Monroe Beardsley's claim regarding unity to the contrary[12]). It may detract from an artwork's interest, especially for those whose tastes tend toward the baroque or richly romantic. Now the fact that 'simple' seems *more* evaluative in science than in art may seem more rather than less of a reason to believe simplicity a real property of artworks. But when 'simple' is used nonevaluatively in application to artworks, the property it signifies is not a typical aesthetic quality, and so an argument for its reality cannot be generalized.

When it is used evaluatively, we again face the problem of disagreement and consequent incoherence in the realist's position, to which we shall return. The third and final question here, however, is whether properties such as simplicity and elegance really are ultimately justificatory criteria for believing theories about the world true. If they were, then realists would have a serious problem, for it would be a serious question for them why we should think that the

world, independent of our belief system as it is, should be elegant
or simple rather than messy and complex. I have proposed a different defense of inference to the best explanation elsewhere, one that
does not rely on a defense of aesthetic criteria for truth.[13] According to this view, we do not justify such inferences by first justifying the separate grounds on which we seem to prefer certain explanatory theories over others. Instead, we argue directly that those
explanations that seem best to us, when inferences to them are
made under favorable conditions, are likely to be approximately
true. We argue this on the ground that it is likely that our brains
have evolved in part for such truth-preserving inferential capacities.[14] "Aesthetic" criteria for theory selection enter the picture
only indirectly, only as rough analogues of what psychologists
could ultimately specify as the more precise grounds on which we
in fact prefer some theories to others.

   If aesthetic criteria are not ultimately justifying for physical theories, then physical realists need not be realists about aesthetic
properties. Scientific theories serve functions that are better served
by theories that strike us as simpler (especially simpler to use).
Artworks are very different in respect to function or lack or it, as
many philosophers, following Kant and British aestheticians before
him, point out. It is not surprising, therefore, that tastes in art vary
far more than tastes in scientific theories. Some prefer the simplicity
of musical minimalism; others prefer Bach's B Minor Mass. These
differences in taste create problems only for aesthetic realism. They
show that purported similarities in criteria for evaluation in the two
domains have been greatly exaggerated. Whatever Keats meant by
his famous last lines on truth and beauty, they have been taken too
literally by some more serious philosophers.

   We may return to the main argument of this section on explanations for agreements and disagreements among art critics. We noted
above an asymmetry in this debate. The nonrealist can explain
agreements without appealing to real properties by citing common
cultural backgrounds and training, resulting in common aesthetic
sensibilities. The realist, however, cannot explain all disagreement
as resulting from deviance from ideal critics or from borderline areas of vague terms. Instead, some disagreement reflects the fact that
differences in taste persist through training and exposure to various
art forms. (By 'taste' here I refer not only to different preferences
but also to different judgments of aesthetic worth that underlie and

reflect those preferences. In some instances preferences and judgments may come apart, but such cases need not concern us here.) Even ideal critics will disagree in their ascriptions of evaluative aesthetic properties because the relevant relations may inform their experiences in different ways and provoke different responses. Or they may place emphasis on different relations at the expense of others. For some music lovers, the formal and expressive properties of pieces by Saint-Saëns give them great aesthetic value; for others, his failure to extend or alter the course of the romantic tradition in an interesting way renders his music insignificant and robs it of aesthetic value.

Although nonrealists have the better of the explanations for agreements and disagreements in ascriptions of aesthetic properties, there remains the question whether they can offer plausible explanations for other phenomena realists seek to explain by appeal to aesthetic properties, for example, explanations of why certain artists paint as they do (to instantiate certain aesthetic properties in their works). If the relational account of aesthetic properties offered above is correct, then these realist explanations appeal to objective properties or lower-order relations that elicit certain (mainly) evaluative responses from a certain privileged class of observers. But then nonrealists can offer very similar explanations in terms of how the artists in question and critics who share their tastes react to various formal and lower-order relations in artworks. According to the nonrealist version, artists paint as they do to create those objective properties that elicit positive reactions from those who share their tastes. Only the last phrase differs from the realist version, and the explanatory force of both explanations is equal despite this difference.

We can now see how nonrealists will modify the relational account of aesthetic properties offered above to avoid the ascription of incompatible properties that plagues the realist. According to the modified account, when I say that an object has a certain aesthetic property, I am saying that ideal critics who generally share my taste will react in a certain way to its more basic properties. When ascriptions of properties are relativized to tastes in this way, the truth of those statements is no longer independent of the ways the properties appear to critics with those tastes. Hence the analysis is no longer realist. Such relativization implies that two critics may not genuinely disagree (except in attitude or response) when one calls

an artwork powerful and the other denies this or calls it merely raucous. But the price of this counterintuitive implication is worth the
gain in avoiding contradiction and explaining away seemingly interminable disagreement among apparently knowledgeable and
sensitive critics. It is because ideal critics can differ in taste that we
must relativize our aesthetic judgments to those ideal critics whose
tastes we share.

Some art viewers or listeners will not have taste shared by any
ideal critic. They certainly will not be reliable judges of artworks.
This does not imply, however, that they can make no true aesthetic
judgments. The lover of only rock music could perhaps nevertheless recognize the power in Beethoven's Ninth should he happen to
hear certain passages from it. He might note truly that these passages are powerful. We can accommodate this recognition on the
present revised account. We need only extrapolate from such judgments to the taste the person would have if he were musically better
trained or experienced. Presumably his judgment about the
Beethoven would remain constant through further training or experience, whereas his judgments of other aesthetic properties of
classical works would not.

Having noted the nonrealist relativism of the new account, we
must also hedge this characterization in closing this section by noting that realism comes in degrees. It comes in degrees because there
are degrees of independence of objects and their properties from
the ways they appear and our beliefs about them and because there
are correlative degrees of agreement and disagreement about when
we are perceiving them. The present account agrees with realism
that the truth of judgments about aesthetic properties is not simply
a matter of how they appear to the critics making these judgments.
They can err in their aesthetic beliefs if they are inattentive, uneducated, biased by personal interest or irrelevant association, or if
their judgments are explained by any other deviation from ideal
critics. Thus in noting the beauty of a Titian painting, I am not simply expressing my own reaction, which I recognize to be fallible,
but expressing my belief that viewers who share my taste but have
no critical defects would concur. I recognize the aesthetic properties of the painting to be independent of my particular responses to
them at a particular viewing. But the truth of such judgments is not
independent of ways they appear to ideal critics, of all evaluative responses to them, or of other aesthetic judgments and beliefs that
constitute different tastes. I implicitly recognize this fact when I

seek out reviews of works by critics whose taste I generally respect and share. In short, judgments that ascribe aesthetic properties to artworks are relative to tastes but still subject to error and illusion. The realist and nonrealist both grasp part but not all of the correct account of these judgments. There is a distinction possible between aesthetic properties and how they appear to us but not between how they are and how they appear to ideal critics of different tastes.

Supervenience and Causality

I can be briefer in discussing another way of characterizing aesthetic judgments in terms of a relation dear to many contemporary philosophers' hearts, that of supervenience. This relation can be defined as follows. When properties of type B supervene on properties of type A, then there cannot be any change or difference in the B properties of objects without some change or difference in their A properties. If two objects are identical in their A properties, then they must be identical in their B properties. The relation is nevertheless weaker than identity or reduction. B properties here are not the same as A properties, and the presence of A properties does not entail the presence of B properties. Supervenience is the relation that is often held to obtain between mental properties (such as sensations) and physical, between moral properties (such as rightness) and nonmoral, and between secondary qualities (such as colors) and physical properties of objects. It is plausible, for example, that humans cannot have different sensations without some difference in their central nervous systems.

Several considerations might suggest that this description also properly characterizes the relation between aesthetic and objective properties of artworks. First, there is the comparison to secondary qualities suggested earlier, qualities that also involve responses of qualified perceivers to objective or physical properties. A parallel to moral properties might also be drawn (to be explored in a later chapter). Second, there is a consideration derived from the artist's point of view. Artists will naturally assume that if they want to change the aesthetic properties of a work in progress, then they must alter its physical properties. How else could a different effect be produced in an audience? Third, we have said that justifying ascriptions of evaluative aesthetic properties always ultimately involves appealing to nonevaluative properties of the objects to which they are ascribed. The aesthetic properties must depend on the nonevaluative properties, and supervenience might be seen as capturing the dependence relation that falls short of entailment.

But even if aesthetic properties as types did supervene on objective properties of artworks, we would need to question first whether this would be relevant to our inquiry. We are interested here in the justification of ascriptions of aesthetic properties, especially evaluative properties, to particular artworks. But it is obvious first of all that those properties of an artwork on which ascriptions of its aesthetic properties depend do not equate with the entire supervenience base for those aesthetic properties. The supervenience base for a given aesthetic property will contain all those nonaesthetic properties that could make a difference to its presence in any context. But an object to which the aesthetic property is ascribed will normally have only a small subset of the supervenience base properties.

Nor is the supervenience base for an aesthetic property a conjunction of all those objective properties that give to all artworks, even all possible artworks, that property. The supervenience base must contain, in addition, all those properties that could cancel or defeat the effects of properties in the conjunctive set just mentioned.[15] These possible defeaters may be boundless in number, and most will seem totally irrelevant to any object's having those qualities that prompt us to ascribe aesthetic properties to it. Containing hyena sounds, for example, is a defeater for the elegance of Mozart's music, and so is part of the supervenience base for that property. In fact, it and countless similarly irrelevant properties enter the supervenience bases for each aesthetic property of every piece of music Mozart composed, since they would change those aesthetic properties were they present in the music.

So far I have been arguing that even if aesthetic properties of artworks did supervene on objective nonaesthetic properties intrinsic to the works, the supervenience bases would be far too wide to be informative about the relations between the aesthetic properties of particular works and those other properties of the works on which they depend (which prompt their ascriptions by ideal critics). But this set of objective properties, even if it contains defeaters in the form of further objective properties possibly contained in the works at given times, is also too narrow to constitute supervenience bases for their aesthetic properties. I shall argue in a later chapter that there are relations of works to both past and sometimes future or later works that help determine what other aesthetic properties they have. Early musical compositions in the classical style were heard as graceful and elegant, and perhaps rightly so, before the works of Haydn and Mozart. But the former works could only be heard as somewhat awkward and groping after the standards for those properties had been forever altered by the fulfillment of classical ideals in the latter works. Most evaluative aesthetic properties are relative in this way to standards that may change with time and new paradigms, although these qualities might not intuitively seem to be so relative. Hence the aesthetic properties of works do not supervene on properties intrinsic to the works themselves. Nevertheless, it is once more those objective properties that prompt critics, including ideal critics, to ascribe aesthetic properties to them.

There are other less subtle relations as well that help to determine aesthetic properties of artworks. A copy that is perceptually indistinguishable from an original painting lacks not only originality and historical importance but may also lack other aesthetic properties of the original: For example, the powerful, expressive qualities of a Van Gogh derived from his agitated brush strokes. Unless we perceive the copy as a Van Gogh, its brush strokes will not be equally expressive. Here we might simply extend the supervenience base from objective properties intrinsic to works so that it includes relations to the historical contexts in which they are created. The supervenience thesis can then survive, although its holders must hope that the broadened supervenience base is still of some interest (remember how broad it must be). But the relations that defeat any interest in supervenience entirely in this context are those most prominent in our analysis of aesthetic properties themselves: relations between an object's other properties and evaluative responses of ideal critics.

From the point of view of the single ideal critic (as from the point of view of the artist), it would seem that evaluative aesthetic properties must supervene on nonevaluative or objective properties of artworks (including now those relations and defeaters noted above). That there can be no difference in ascriptions of evaluative properties without some difference in objective properties amounts to a constraint on rational aesthetic judgment that an ideal critic would satisfy. Her evaluative judgment would remain constant in the face of the same nonevaluative properties, given her fully developed taste and knowledge of all historical relations that contribute to or detract from an artwork's worth. This constraint might not be met by ordinary viewers of art, whose tastes change and develop and who therefore change their evaluations of similar or identical works. Might not an ideal critic too tire of viewing some work and therefore change his evaluation of it? No, since, being omniscient of the relevant relations, he would know from the beginning how well the work would withstand sustained viewing.

Since the possession of aesthetic properties by works depends on the responses of ideal and not ordinary critics, supervenience on a suitably broadened base of objective properties might still seem to hold. It seems to hold because the ideal critic seems to be under the same constraint as the moral judge: not to judge cases differently without some relevant nonevaluative difference between them. But the crucial point once more is that even fully developed and informed tastes can differ across ideal critics. Supervenience therefore fails. Irreconcilable differences in taste imply that ascriptions of aesthetic properties such as grace or garishness will differ in regard to the same artworks, therefore, when objective properties remain constant. Supervenience fails precisely because such ascriptions are ineliminably evaluative, or at the least involve subjective responses, without our being constrained to reconcile our differences, as we are in moral judgment.

Secondary qualities such as color are also relations ineliminably involving subjective responses or ways of appearing. But they do supervene on physical properties of objects if normal perceivers sense them similarly. Since colors are typed according to how they appear, and since it is conceivable that physical properties could appear differently in regard to color, colors cannot be reduced, type-identified with, or conceptually connected with their physical bases. We might token identify particular instantiations of color with the physical properties that appear colored in those instances, but the supervenience relation seems optimal for describing the relation between colors as universals or types and those configurations of molecules on the surfaces of objects that appear to us colored. Not so when describing the relation between aesthetic and nonaesthetic properties of objects.

Why could we not simply expand the supervenience base once more to include the responses of ideal critics? We then finally would seem to satisfy the criterion for supervenience. But there would be no point at all in mentioning this relation for two obvious reasons. First, aesthetic properties would not simply supervene on relations between objective properties of works and responses of ideal critics: As our original account maintains, they reduce to those relations, eliminating the need to speak of supervenience. Second, the relations in which we are interested are precisely those just mentioned. We want to know how and why ideal critics respond as they do to properties of various artworks in order to know which aesthetic properties those works have and how those qualities emerge from the objective properties of the works. Talk of supervenience tells us nothing of this. As Kant intimated in denying that we can conceptualize the objective grounds of beauty, those properties of particular works that determine their separate aesthetic qualities are likely to be more or less uniquely instantiated in those works. One painting is beautiful because of its unique form; another is beautiful because of its highly unusual combination of vivid colors. If we can generalize from such particular cases to say anything interesting about the sources of aesthetic value, it will not be from knowledge of supervenience bases but from reflection on a narrower class of higher-order properties and the responses they cause.

In this chapter I have been mainly concerned with metaphysics, with the ontology of aesthetic properties. I will turn to more direct discussion of the epistemology of aesthetic evaluation in later chapters. Our discussion of realism in the previous section, however, was relevant to the justification of evaluative aesthetic judgments by appeal to nonevaluative properties of artworks. If evaluative aesthetic properties were real, then on the one hand we could be more easily mistaken in our ascriptions of them. But, on the other hand, we could then identify tokens or instantiations of them with those properties of works to which we respond in ascribing the aesthetic qualities to them. Knowledge of the objective properties would suffice, given knowledge of these identities, for knowing the aesthetic properties of particular works. Realism turned out to be untenable, and so our epistemology will need to be more complex. Aesthetic judgments, or ascriptions of evaluative aesthetic properties, must be relativized to tastes.

The question of supervenience has no similarly relevant implications, since, as we have seen, even if aesthetic properties did supervene on nonaesthetic properties of artworks, the base would be so broad as to lack epistemological interest. But the discussion was important for introducing contrasts between aesthetic judgments, judgments regarding secondary qualities, and moral judgments. Secondary qualities, we have seen, are more easily considered real properties of physical objects than are aesthetic qualities. And the former do seem to supervene on physical properties. Moral properties such as rightness, like aesthetic qualities, are not real properties of objects or actions. But moral judgments differ from aesthetic judgments in such a way as to make moral properties seem also to supervene on nonmoral properties. One is not to judge moral cases differently without being able to cite some relevant generalizable nonmoral difference between them. When I further compare aesthetic to moral judgments in a later chapter, I shall argue that this constraint does not apply in the domain of aesthetic judgments. These contrasts are instructive for appreciating the nature of aesthetic properties as well as the epistemology of aesthetic judgments, since in all these cases we find relations between objective properties and responses of certain designated subjects.

Evaluative aesthetic properties, I have argued, are not identical to, conceptually or definitionally connected with, or supervenient on nonevaluative properties of artworks or other objects. Yet aesthetic judgments ascribing such properties are justified by appeal to nonevaluative base properties on which evaluative aesthetic properties depend. The dependence relation was actually indicated in our initial analysis of aesthetic properties: It is causal. As noted there, ascriptions of aesthetic properties are true, relative to certain tastes, when base properties of artworks cause certain responses in critics with ideal characteristics. Such judgments are justified when we are justified in ascribing these causal relations. Our next task, then, is to specify the base (or nonevaluative) aesthetic properties and to describe how and why they cause the evaluative responses they do.

CHAPTER THREE

Base Properties

In the previous chapter it was held that evaluative aesthetic properties are constituted ultimately by relations between nonevaluative properties of artworks, which we can call base properties, and positive or negative reactions of certain observers. The base properties themselves may be relational, but they are not relations to these evaluative reactions. Instead, they constitute the objective components of evaluative aesthetic properties. In this chapter we must specify the nature of these base properties and inquire how and why they cause such reactions in ideal critics, that is, why they are sources of value in artworks. To do so we may return to our original list of typical aesthetic properties provided at the beginning of the previous chapter, and we must ask of the base properties underlying each type the two questions indicated: What is their nature? and Why are they of value? Once we have the answer to these two questions, we will understand the major sources of aesthetic value.

It was noted earlier that the first type of property on the list, the broadly evaluative properties such as beauty, may rest on different sorts of lower-level properties. A work may be beautiful by virtue of its elegance or its stark power, for example. Elegance in turn is an evaluative formal property, whereas powerful works are typically highly expressive. In other similar cases too the narrower evaluative properties on which the broader ones immediately depend in turn depend on nonevaluative formal or expressive qualities. The next four categories on the list—formal, emotion, evocative, and behavioral qualities—once again involve reactions to nonevaluative formal properties or to those typically described as expressive, with the addition now of representational content to the base. Works may express sadness, anger, or jauntiness without being representational, but they are typically amusing or hilarious because of their

45

represented content (not always, since certain musical turns of phrase, in pieces by Haydn or Rossini, for example, can be amusing in themselves by virtue of their formal or expressive qualities). The sixth category on the list contains qualities of representations; the seventh, sensuous qualities (described in evaluative terms); and the eighth, evaluations of relations of works to their historical traditions.

Base properties, then, seem to be formal, expressive, representational (including symbolic), sensuous, and historical properties of works. I shall discuss historical relations and their effects on value in a later chapter. Sensuous qualities merit little discussion here, since in this context we may take it as a brute fact that certain types of sensations or sensuous qualities of tones or colors are pleasing (although only in certain combinations and to certain subjects).[1] What remain for our concern in this chapter are expressive, representational, and formal qualities of works. We need to know how artworks attain these properties—what it means to say that a work expresses so and so or what the criteria are for a work's representing x rather than y—and why works that have these qualities might be evaluated positively on that basis. Why are highly expressive pieces of music, such as the overture to *The Barber of Seville* or the slow movement of Mahler's Fifth Symphony, thought to be good at least partly on that ground? Why is representation in painting, what Plato called a mere imitation of an imitation (or appearance), a source of aesthetic value? And what do we mean by ascribing formal perfection to the opening movement of a Haydn string quartet? I shall begin the answers to these questions with a discussion of artistic expression.

Expression

We generally think of music as the expressive art form par excellence. Prior to the nineteenth century, when art in general was conceptualized as primarily representational, music was not of primary importance to philosophers of aesthetics. But with the rise of romanticism and its emphasis on the artist's personal expression of unique emotional states, music came to the fore in aesthetic theory. Yet although there can be no doubt that musical pieces are described as expressing human, and especially emotional, states, and although many pieces are praised for their expressive power or clarity, it is precisely in relation to music that it is most difficult to answer our two questions. Controversy continues among philosophers of music about what it means to say that a piece expresses emotion and how sequences of tones achieve this effect. Although the topic is less widely discussed, it is also puzzling why, in general, the fact that emotion and other human-quality terms seem apt for describing certain pieces or passages should indicate some positive value that we find in them. This may be especially puzzling in the particular case that does draw attention, when the emotion expressed in a piece is one we normally would rather avoid, such as sadness.

The main debate here pits communication or arousal theorists, who hold that music is sad, joyful, or angry by communicating or arousing like states in listeners, against cognitivists, who claim that we recognize analogues of these states in music without feeling them ourselves while listening. The classic theory of the first type is Tolstoy's, according to which an artist feels a certain emotion and communicates it to an audience by arousing the same state in them via the artwork.[2] In its favor is first the fact that the very concept of expression strongly suggests the model of someone's expressing some feeling to someone else. If there is to be genuine expression, then must there not be someone who is expressing something he feels in a way that affects the person to whom it is expressed? Second, we seem to ascribe emotion terms to both causes and effects of emotions as well as to the states themselves. For example, we talk of sad events and sad demeanors. According to this theory we call music sad because it is both an effect and a cause of sadness, and this seems to fit with other ordinary uses of this term. Third, Tolstoy's theory appears to have a clear answer to our second question. According to him, art, as opposed to ordinary language, is peculiarly apt for communicating feeling (as opposed to thought), and this communication creates bonds among people that are clearly of human value, especially when the feelings transmitted are of an ennobling kind.

Despite these attractions, there are overwhelming and obvious objections to the theory in regard to both the nature and value of expression. Regarding the second point above, one can respond that we do not ascribe emotion terms to all causes and effects of emotions but only to their objects and expressions (e.g., events and demeanors).[3] Music is not the object of sadness—we are not sad about

the music. And whether it is an effect of its composer's sadness is irrelevant to what the work expresses to an audience. In the next
chapter on interpretation we will encounter the argument that an
artist's intended meaning must be irrelevant to what her work
means since if she successfully conveys what she intends, then the
intention will be evident in the work itself. And if the intention is
unfulfilled or unsuccessfully conveyed, then it is once more irrelevant to what the work itself means. Whatever the merits of this argument, which remain to be briefly examined later, it is less com-
pelling than the parallel point made in regard to artists' feelings
when they create. Although we might be inclined to change our
guess as to what an obscure literary work means upon finding that
its author could not have intended any such thing, we would not
change our characterization in expressive terms of Mozart's sunny
Nineteenth Piano Concerto or of his brooding and passionate
Twentieth if we should find that he was depressed when writing the
former (or even that depression caused him to write it) and cheerful
in composing the latter.[4] This last point contrasts artistic expression
with natural expressions of emotions in people's faces or behavior.
If we learn that a person is not sad, then we no longer take his
droopy face and slow gait to express sadness. By contrast, attribut-
ing a feeling to an artist cannot be part of what it means to say that
his work expresses that feeling.

This conclusion should not be taken too broadly. Although expressive artworks do not necessarily express their creators' feelings
or emotions, they do often express other traits, especially long-term
character traits, of their creators. No one who knows Rossini's
works can doubt that he possessed great wit, and this is evident
from his music itself, independent of the texts. But the certainty
with which we can infer the character trait from the music exists
partly because wittiness, as opposed to such mental states as emotions or feelings, is just a disposition to make witty remarks or in
this case artworks. Certain other characterizations of artworks
seem to imply certain intentional states in their artists. If a work is
ironic, then it seems that the artist must have been ironic in her creation of it or treatment of its subject. This claim remains to be evaluated in terms of a broader theory of interpretation in the next
chapter, however. It is not necessarily true, since even if we accept
that irony requires someone's being ironic, we can always attribute
irony in a literary work to a fictional narrator instead of an author.

And even if we accept the claim in the end, we can take it once more to mark a contrast between irony and emotional states that artworks can express. Our conclusion regarding emotional states might be challenged by arguing that although composers need not be sad in order to compose sad music, the latter is the sort of music that sad composers would produce if they wished to express their feelings through their music. But this is to say no more than that if they want to express sadness, then they must make this evident in their works, which applies to cheerful composers also.

There are nevertheless cases in which features of works reflect creative acts that seem indissolubly linked to emotional states of their creators. A prime example is the aforementioned agitated brush strokes of Van Gogh, which both express agitation in his works and seem so immediately revealing of an agitated psyche. I allowed earlier that a copy of a Van Gogh is not similarly expressive to us once we know that the brush strokes themselves are copied. This would seem to indicate that the absence of the requisite emotional state in the artist is relevant to the expressive quality of the work, contradicting our present claim. But two points can be combined in reply to this case. First, although an intent merely to copy may cancel many expressive qualities of the product (just as an accidental natural object formally identical to an artwork might not express the same), this does not imply that each expressive quality of a work depends on a like mental state in its creator. The claim still holds that such states are normally irrelevant. Second, in the case mentioned, our independent knowledge of Van Gogh's personality and mental problems makes his paintings seem so much an expression of his troubled mental states. In this case I believe that if we had knowledge instead that Van Gogh had a stable and cheerful disposition, we would interpret his brush strokes as expressive of some state other than anguish, perhaps bold exuberance. But we cannot generalize from this case, as is clear from other cases, such as Mozart's, which involve different relations of artists to their works. That Van Gogh's artistic style seems to match his personality so well suggests in *that* case that the expressive qualities of his works depend on their causal relations to his mental states, but we often find no such relations in the case of Mozart and other great artists.

Returning to the narrower domain of music, it remains to ask whether a musical work's arousing an emotion in its audience is part of the concept of expression or the means by which we must

identify expressive qualities. Again the answer appears to be negative. A work that I recognize to be sad need not make me sad when
I listen to it if, for example, I am in an irrepressibly cheerful mood.
This objection can be met by speaking instead of a work's tendency
to affect its audience affectively. But once more its tendency to
cause an emotion in its audience cannot be necessary or sufficient
for characterizing a piece as expressive of that emotion. It cannot be
sufficient because a work may tend to make an audience sad or angry because of how pitifully bad it is, how lacking altogether in expressive power. Indeed, an audience is more likely to be made angry
by a poor work than by one recognizably expressive of anger or
naturally characterized as angry. A work's tendency to arouse a
feeling cannot be necessary for its expressing that feeling because
we can recognize expressive qualities in works without ever experiencing the like emotions, just as we can recognize a weeping willow
tree or a bloodhound's face as expressive of sadness without being
made sad by seeing them. The last example is from Peter Kivy, who
is clearly good at identifying expressive qualities in musical pieces
but denies that expressive pieces, especially those expressing negative or unpleasant emotions, tend to make him feel that way (at
least he denies that this tendency is ever actually realized in him). If
such pieces did make him feel that way, he maintains, then he
would not want to listen to them.[5]

   That arousing an emotion is neither necessary nor sufficient for
expressing that emotion leaves open the question whether music
can and sometimes does arouse emotional reactions and also
whether its doing so might sometimes be a criterion for its expressing emotions. Here there can be no doubt that the answer to the
first question is affirmative. The widespread and effective use of
music in all societies for ritualistic, ceremonial, political, and military occasions would be largely inexplicable if it did not have the
effect of arousing and coordinating emotional reactions of social
groups, aiding them in or preparing them for communal actions.
There is much other evidence also for causal relations of music to
emotional states. Its therapeutic effects are well known to clinical
psychologists and to ordinary listeners. Its bodily effects are easily
measured. Its rhythms stimulate bodily movements, sometimes ir-
resistibly, some of which themselves naturally express emotional
states as well. Animals and infants react affectively to intensity,
pitch, and rhythm in the human voice without understanding con-

tent, and these are musical characteristics. Finally, just as certain colors and color combinations can "set a mood," so different harmonic combinations and developments can provoke affective reactions. All this evidence leaves little question that music can have these effects, although the precise states that can be aroused and the means by which they are aroused can still be a matter of debate.

In regard to the types of affective states aroused, debate centers on whether these are ordinary garden-variety emotions or feelings peculiar to the experience of listening to music. No one disputes that the latter feelings are crucial to listening to music with understanding. Musical forms, as these combine harmonic, rhythmic, and melodic elements, are heard and often identified through developing affect. Formal developments that are not yet complete—for example, harmonic progression from tonic or subdominant to dominant or regularly rising melodic patterns—create expectations for further development and resolution. These expectations are felt as tensions, and the affective effect is heightened by delay or prolongation of the fulfillment of expectation or closure.[6] Those who appreciate music do not listen passively and passionlessly. They actively listen for what is to come in light of what has been foretold, pointed ahead by the unfolding progressions. The listener absorbed in a piece becomes like an agent whose will is involved in pursuit of the musical goals defined by these patterns of building tension and release. The affective states internal to the perception of music may be more or less unique, but they are most like those that arise in the course of contested goal-directed action.

I said that cognitivists about expressive qualities in music need not deny that these feelings internal to the proper perception of musical pieces are aroused in the course of listening. Nor do they deny another sort of affective state that may be aroused. Cognitivists, like other music lovers, may be moved by the beauty of a piece or a performance or even by the beautiful way in which a piece expresses some garden-variety emotion.[7] What they deny is that such an emotion is expressed via its arousal in listeners. They deny this on a variety of grounds, two of which were mentioned earlier: that listeners would not want to hear sad or angry music if it were true and that musical pieces do not provide objects to which ordinary emotions can attach, as they ordinarily do.[8] If a piece of music expresses anger or sadness, we are not angry at the piece or sad about it. If emotions require both objects and appropriate beliefs about them, and they often are differentiated in these ways, then music does not seem capable of arousing them.

This last argument is answered by denying that the antecedent of the previous sentence is true of all emotions. We are sometimes sad or angry without knowing what we are sad or angry about. The cause may be a hormonal reaction rather than an object, in which case there may be nothing we are sad or angry about. Only some emotions can lack objects, however. They are characterized as moods and can be differentiated solely according to their feeling tones and/or behavioral manifestations. There may be no difference in feeling between jealousy and contempt, but there does seem to be a feeling unique to sadness. And anger, unlike jealousy and contempt, is typically manifested in particular patterns of agitated or violent behavior. The noteworthy fact here is that those emotions that can be differentiated without having objects or beliefs about them are precisely the ones that music is ordinarily said to express—such states as sadness or anger but not jealousy or contempt (without accompanying texts or programs). This fact defeats this argument against the claim that music expresses these emotions by arousing them in listeners.

Kivy's latest argument against the arousal theory is that it provides no explanation for how music can arouse ordinary emotions, no indication of the method by which it does this.[9] The usual way in which such emotions are aroused is once more via an object to which certain affectively charged beliefs refer. The absence of objects to which the arousal theory can appeal enters this argument in a new way, as removing the possibility for a plausible explanation of means or method. In other cases in which objectless emotions occur, we can assume that these states are caused by objects (or memories of objects) of which the subjects are not presently conscious or by some direct chemical reactions in their nervous systems. But these causes seem equally irrelevant to any plausible explanation of how music is supposed to arouse ordinary emotions.

The cognitivist, by contrast, claims to have an explanation for how we come to recognize expressive properties in music, how we come to describe musical passages in emotion terms without feeling the emotions. The main basis for this recognition is the resemblance of the music in its pitch, volume, and rhythmic and melodic contours to the natural expressions of emotion in voice, demeanor, and behavior. Thus sad music tends to be low, soft, and slow, perhaps including descending sequences of tones, and angry music tends to be higher pitched and loud, with rapid and unpredictable rhythms and sharp breaks in melodic contour. Literal imitation is only of the voice; bodily movements are not heard, but the same predicates apply to them and to "movement" in music. The scare quotes indicate that musical movement itself is not literal movement through space. Notes are not spatially higher or lower, except in scores. Part (but only part) of what makes it so natural to use spatial terms in describing pitch and progressions of tones may be that higher notes seem to require more energy (perhaps this claim reflects only the bias of an old trumpet player for whom it is literally true), just as it requires more energy to move to higher spatial positions. This suggestion, and the general spatial descriptive framework for music, connect once more to the ascription of certain emotional qualities, since, for example, sad people not only speak in low tones but also generally lack energy and move more slowly whereas angry people tend to be animated and energetic. Once we accept spatial descriptions of notes, description as movement follows, since change of spatial position is perceived as movement. Once we describe music as moving, we can compare it to human movements that naturally express emotion (variants of which the music can also directly stimulate by its rhythm).

This account is plausible as far as it goes. Surely the association between the features of music mentioned and vocal and behavioral expressions of emotion is not merely coincidental or conventional. It is no real objection that we notice emotional properties in music without noticing the analogies to voice or behavior,[10] since we often apply terms without being aware of the criteria by which we are doing so (otherwise, analytic philosophy would be far easier). But the account is also incomplete and problematic as part of an attack on the arousal theory. It is incomplete because it contains no explanation for the difference in emotional tone between major and minor keys, for example. The cognitivist must hold that the association of minor keys with sadness or negative emotional states is purely conventional, but this claim is no more plausible than a corresponding allegation in regard to dull and muted versus bright and saturated colors. If colors express certain moods by arousing them, and these connections are not merely conventional, why should not the same be true of tonal harmonies?

The other problem for the resemblance account is that many things other than expressions of emotion resemble musical contours, rhythms, and volumes. Many things, for example, move

slowly and even emit low and soft sounds without being associated
with music that has these qualities. Kivy has a response to this objection. We naturally pick out human emotional states for association from among all the phenomena that resemble music in these
ways because of our innate tendency to animate perceived phenomena, to view them in human terms.[11] A weeping willow or a bloodhound's face looks sad to us, although they could equally be associated with many other objects or shapes that droop. This tendency
toward anthropomorphic categorization, well evidenced especially
in children, can in turn be explained in terms of the biological and
psychological centrality of human relations to us.

Again the explanation is plausible if highly speculative. The
problem for Kivy as a cognitivist is that it is just as plausible that we
are wired not only to animate what we perceive but also to react
emotively to recognition of human-type states in perceived phenomena. Once more this reaction will not be based on a conscious
process of inference or a drawing of analogy. If it were, then our
knowledge that musical pieces are not sentient would block an affective response to music. But such recognition would equally
block the initial ascription of emotion predicates to music if that
were based on conscious inference or analogizing. If, therefore,
Kivy's own explanation for recognition of emotional states in music, appealing as it does to biologically wired dispositions, can be
plausibly extended to explain the disposition to be affectively
aroused by the same pieces, then his latest objection to the arousal
theory collapses.[12]

It is plausible, once again given the importance of human relations and the emotional ties that they require, that we naturally react both sympathetically and empathically to the recognition of human emotional states. Thus, for example, we might react to the
recognition of sadness with either sadness of our own or pity or
both. Since pity requires an object, however, it must be sadness
rather than pity that is aroused by sad musical pieces. But isn't this
claim contradicted by the fact that seeing bloodhounds and weeping willows does not tend to make us sad? There may be several differences between these cases and the perception of emotional states
in music. First, it may be that weeping willows do tend to provoke
at least a mild wistfulness, which, however, wears off with complete
familiarity, much as a piece of music we have heard ten thousand
times loses its expressive power for us (unlike other pieces). Second,

although, as argued above, we need not attribute to its real composer the emotional states that we ascribe to a musical work, we do
tend to perceive such works as human expressions, unlike natural
objects such as trees or animals. Perceiving music as a human product makes it more likely that we react to it affectively.

I am suggesting that both theories of the nature of musical expression are compatible and equally believable. It is furthermore
likely that recognition and arousal of emotional states interact and
reinforce one another in listening to music. We might be affected
emotionally by the recognition of some structural features of natural
expression in music, and we might in turn recognize such features
more readily when we begin to feel their effects. Factors that contribute directly to affective reactions, such as minor tonalities, are insufficient in themselves to produce this effect, but it seems clear that
they operate together with recognitional factors to prompt affective
responses from listeners. If music did not arouse as well as represent
emotional states (or close analogues to them), if, as Kivy maintains,
we were moved only by the beautiful way in which certain pieces
capture certain emotions, then we would be moved in the same way
by great music that is cheerful and sad music, in the same way by the
overture to *The Barber of Seville* and by the slow movement to
Mahler's Fifth Symphony.[13] Kivy responds that such pieces instantiate different sorts of beauty, and so our response to their beauty is
not the same.[14] But it seems to me that our responses are not the
same because they are at least typically mixed with something like
exuberance in the one case and sorrow in the other.

Thus the base properties for relational expressive properties can
take a variety of forms, even when we confine attention to music
alone. They can be structural or formal features of melody and/or
rhythm that resemble natural expression of emotion in voice or behavior, or they can be harmonic properties that directly stimulate
affective reactions in the proper contexts (changes in volume can
fall into both categories). There are also conventional factors mentioned above only in passing: relations to texts, programs or titles,
or stylistic conventions such as the association of horns, especially
in romantic music, with expansive feelings for the outdoors. We
must add causal relations to the base properties to get full-blown
expressive properties: The former cause the proper listeners to ascribe emotion predicates either via recognition or affective reaction
or, most commonly, both.

Without doing violence to our linguistic use or intuitions we can identify instances of these properties with the base properties that cause the expressive ascriptions or reactions in the particular cases. A piece of music's being sad consists in its being such as to elicit these responses, and the "being such" can be identified in particular works with base properties of the types specified above. But use of emotion terms and reference to affective reactions cannot be eliminated for at least two reasons. First, they are ineliminable from the epistemic viewpoint of listeners, since they ascribe emotion properties to music without normally conceptualizing the objective bases on which they do so. Second, as I will argue further below, reference to emotion-type reactions is crucial for understanding the value of expressive properties in artworks. Our sense of the tragic and our affective reaction to it are necessary to a full appreciation of the adagietto movement of Mahler's Fifth Symphony, although we can identify these particular instances of such expressive properties with the long-lined melodies of the movement, its excruciatingly drawn-out harmonic suspensions, and its muted volumes punctuated by simmering crescendos.

When we speak of types of expressive properties instead of instances (instantiations), the neatest relation we can have of these properties to their bases is one-many, since, as we have seen, there are many combinations of base properties of different kinds that can prompt ascriptions of such properties as sadness. With such broadly specified mood properties as sadness or anger, the relation may well be one-many, because qualified listeners may well agree on their presence in various musical passages. But if instead we think of melancholic versus funereal versus anguished, or furious versus stormy versus sullen (we have ruled out such descriptions as contemptuous), then such agreement may vanish, and the relation of bases to subjective reactions and full-blown expressive properties becomes more complex.

Here we can ask, as we will ask later in regard to purer evaluations, whether these relations can be captured by principles. Is it the case that whenever music has certain base (objective) properties, it also has or tends to have (has in the absence of defeaters) certain expressive or emotion properties? One might think that since the relation between base and full-blown expressive properties is causal (the base properties cause certain qualified listeners to recognize emotion and react), the answer must be affirmative. This might seem to follow from the fact that causes require laws or principles. But, although we may assume that there are psychophysical laws of the kind required here, the problem is that the causal relations in question may differ from individual listener to listener. Once more the lack of objective grounds for agreement in ascribing specific emotion properties to music blocks not only type identification of these properties with their bases but also principles that could capture the relation between them. Nevertheless, the skeptical conclusion must be accepted here only for the narrower emotion properties as opposed to the ascription of broadly specified moods. It is also the case that the more composers combine bases (harmonic, rhythmic, melodic, loudness) for ascribing specific emotion properties to their pieces, the more circumscribed we are (and less skeptical we need be) in describing and reacting to the pieces in these terms.

I have argued that we do, although we need not, react affectively to the recognition of emotion properties in music and that such reaction enters into the explanation for the value of these expressive properties. It remains to specify that explanation. But first a further concession to the cognitivist must be made explicit. In noting that our affective reactions to music lack objects and the typical beliefs of ordinary emotional states I have conceded that these reactions are not ordinary emotions. They also lack the typical motivations to behavior of ordinary emotions (although some behavioral manifestations can be imitated in the music)—to flee from, or offer aid to, or strike the object of one's ordinary emotions. I have maintained that they consist instead of feelings or sensations characteristic of certain emotional states, in this case arising not from usual objects or beliefs but from recognition of analogues of natural expressions of like states in the music.

If we think that emotions must include cognitive states or analogues to them, then we will be inclined to substitute for genuine beliefs other cognitive or quasi-cognitive states in analyzing affective reactions to artworks. This is what Kendall Walton and those who follow his theory of artistic representations and expression do. According to him, we do not experience real emotions in attending to art or music, but it is fictional or make-believe that we experience such emotions.[15] This amounts to the claim that we experience the feelings, as I have maintained, but that these result from our recognition that we are to imagine the contents of the beliefs that would ordinarily give rise to the full-blown emotions. For example, in a horror movie we recognize that it is fictional that the monster is lurking about (we are to imagine that he is, according to the rules of the fictional game that the movie establishes), and this recognition and imagination (as opposed to belief) causes the sensations of fear and thus makes it make-believe that we are afraid. This theory provides answers to certain puzzles, for example, why lovers of tragedy feel sympathy for the hero but still want the play to end tragically. The answer lies in the claim that it is only fictional that they sympathize with the hero. Despite its virtues, however, the theory cannot be generalized to all our affective reactions to art. It specifically does not apply to music, despite Walton's claim to the contrary.

Paradigm emotional states involve objects, beliefs about them, motivational effects or behavioral dispositions, and associated sensations and/or physiological effects. Deviations from the paradigms may vary along any of these dimensions. According to Walton, the subject reacting to art lacks the beliefs and motivations of real emotions, substitutes imagination for belief, and experiences the typical sensations, making the subject's states make-believe rather than real emotions. But, on the one hand, real emotions, we have noted, can lack objects, and they can also lack the beliefs and motivations of their more ordinary counterparts. Phobias involve fearing what their subjects do not believe to be really dangerous, and we may pity victims of a distant disaster without being motivated to aid or comfort them. On the other hand, some viewers of horror movies might be disposed to flinch, block out the monster from view, or even to flee from the theater (although they usually suppress the latter motivation). And we would intuitively think of make-believe emotions, as in children's games, as involving some of the behavioral dispositions of real emotions but without the real sensations that Walton takes to be included in our affective reactions to art.

Returning to the domain of music, the question for Walton's theory is what we could be imagining when listening to music that would produce the sensations involved in what he characterizes as make-believe emotions. One possibility would be that we imagine that the music is an expression by the composer of his emotion (what Tolstoy's theory held to be literally true). The easiest way to do this would be to imagine that the music is a voice expressing emotion, since the voice is the closest natural means of expression.

But instrumental music is still not much like a real voice expressing anger or any other emotion, so the task for imagination would be formidable. More to the point, it is unnecessary, since we can recognize structural analogues of natural expressions and ascribe emotion properties to music without performing this feat of imagination. Certainly we can react affectively without the superfluous imaginary object, as is clear from the fact that we react to harmonic keys or chords, which we do not typically imagine to be other than they are.

Walton's own choice of imaginary object for the music listener is not the human voice. Instead he claims that we pretend to introspect directly our own emotions when listening to expressive pieces. The meaning of this claim is not clear. Is it that we pretend to experience certain emotions and to attend to them at the same time? Doing so might make it difficult to attend to the music. Walton suggests, perhaps to keep our attention anchored to the music in his analysis, that we imagine that our own auditory sensations when listening are emotions.[16] But I must confess to difficulty in even understanding this possibility. I know that I do not attempt this imaginative feat when listening to music, and I find no evidence that others do so, other than the very fact that they ascribe expressive properties to the passages they hear. Only the assumption that there must be cognitive or quasi-cognitive states included as aspects of emotions or their art viewer analogues could motivate the ascription of these states of imagination. But we have seen that that assumption does not always hold even in cases of real emotions (such as objectless anger or phobia).

In my view it is generally less perspicuous to say that we have imaginary emotions in reacting to art than to say that we react emotionally to the imaginary worlds of the artworks. We do not imagine that we are sad, but we have feelings of sadness in the contexts of the works' worlds (the latter metaphor will be cashed out later, but it applies to musical works as well). Since when attending to a work we remain aware of the artistic medium even while reacting affectively (and must remain aware of the medium if we are to appreciate the work fully), we are normally not disposed to act in response (we can act only in the real world). But neither are we emotionally detached from the world of the artwork. Arousal theorists hold that artworks cause ordinary emotions; cognitivists see nothing like ordinary emotion in our reactions (except in our reaction to beauty or skill). The correct middle view is that emotions, albeit not ordinary or paradigm ones, do occur in the full engagement of an audience with a work, especially with many musical works. The unusual features of these emotions (or their lack of usual features) are explained not by the fact that we only imagine experiencing them but rather by our experiencing them in the context of being engaged in other ways as well with the works to which we react. Full appreciation normally requires some attention to form, for example, as well as affective reaction, and attention to such other matters is sufficient to block full-blown emotional reactions.

I have claimed that the cognitivist cannot explain the value of expressive properties in music. We do not listen, for example, to acquire knowledge of our emotions or affective life, to achieve some kind of self-understanding. Some have held that music provides a map of the way our emotional states change and develop; others claim that music can capture nuances among emotions that language cannot adequately describe. But the map provided by musical works could not be very accurate, since, for one thing, expressive qualities change in music far more rapidly than do emotions in real life. And, as I indicated above, language is, if anything, more capable than music of differentiating emotional states, since language can describe the objects and beliefs by which such states are often differentiated. To learn human psychology we would do better to study literature than music, since the former can specify the objects and causes of our emotions in as much detail as authors care to provide. Or, perhaps better still, we should study psychology itself. Indeed, if we did not recognize analogues of expressions of particular emotions in musical passages, we could not recognize expressive properties in the music. Since we must know of the real emotions before such recognition occurs, it is doubtful that this recognition could teach us anything about the emotions.

Kivy holds that expressive properties function in music as additional formal elements and that their value lies therein.[17] But, compared to melodic phrases and harmonic chords, for example, there are too few readily identifiable elements and too little opportunity for variation, development, and combination for expressive properties to be very valuable in this regard. It was noted above that the classic arousal theory, by contrast, does have an explanation for the value of expressive properties. According to it, the communication of emotions allows individuals to share their affective lives and to improve them through the arousal of the noblest kinds of emotional states.

But this theory faces telling objections in this area as well. Many great musical pieces and other artworks communicate mainly negative emotions rather than noble ones. And if the artwork is merely a means to the communication or arousal of specific emotional states, and if this source of value is, as it were, detachable from any other kinds of worth the work might possess, then any other means of expressing the same states, if equally effective in arousing them, must be equally valuable. Not only would there be nothing uniquely valuable about art in this regard, but more direct means of communicating or arousing anger or fear, for example, would have to count as better. Arousing emotion cannot therefore be the primary end in itself of art, musical or otherwise. It might be claimed that art (or music) is uniquely apt for arousing emotions or that it is able to arouse unique emotional states, but there is no evidence in regard to either claim that art can accomplish what real life cannot.

The arousal of negative emotions has been noted as a problem for the classic arousal theory, but indeed it is a problem for any arousal theory, as Kivy emphasizes. Throughout the history of aesthetics, beginning with Aristotle, there has been no shortage of attempts to dismiss the negative and account for the positive value of such arousal. Explanations for our enjoyment of works that express and arouse negative emotions include Aristotle's idea of catharsis, the claim that what we enjoy is the artistic skill involved in the expression, the claim that we enjoy the lack of real objects or threats connected with these emotions in real life, and the idea that we gain mastery over them or reassurance in our own sensitivities from experiencing them in the context of art.[18] None of these explanations is without serious problems, however.

The idea of catharsis, or release, as the value of negative emotions in art assumes that these emotions exist in us and need release, whether or not they are caused by real-life situations, and that their release in viewing art is either enjoyable in itself or mitigates their harmful effects when they do occur in real life. To my knowledge these assumptions lack convincing psychological evidence. The claim that we enjoy the skill with which artists capture these emotions may be sometimes true, but it fails to explain why many viewers enjoy junk horror movies or pulp novels, for example. This thesis makes it seem as if we endure the negative emotions to appreciate the skill, but many seem to enjoy the experience itself within the artistic context. Similarly, the lack of real objects and threats once more may help to explain our endurance of these emotion properties in art, but not their value. Turning to the final claim, there is no evidence that music or art lovers master their emotions better or are more sensitive than others. The idea that one can be reassured of one's sensitivity by listening to music (as opposed to empathizing with other real people) is strange at best and implausibly egotistical as an explanation for the value of expressive properties. In regard to mastery, if we seek to master our reactions by maintaining full control over them while experiencing art, this may eliminate or dampen the affective response that is supposed to be of value. If the sense of mastery is to derive instead from the overcoming of negative emotions in the course of works themselves (and hence in the course of experiencing them), then this sense (of relief as much as mastery) might be part of a full explanation of our enjoyment of some works. But since we do not normally seek out negative experiences simply to enjoy the relief from their coming to an end, this once more cannot constitute a full explanation for the value of negative emotion properties in artworks.

It is a main thesis of this chapter that we cannot provide a full explanation for the values of the different kinds of base properties if we consider them in isolation from the others and from the way they contribute together to the overall value of artworks. This claim is perhaps most obviously true of negative emotion properties, but it is more broadly true of our affective reactions in general to works of art. These reactions are part of our full involvement with artworks, especially challenging works. Such involvement also includes our cognitive capacities in appreciating form and content as well as our imaginations. Only in the context of our full appreciation of various works can we understand the contributions of the separate sources of value.

I claimed above that to be engaged with a piece of music is at least to be caught up in the affects internal to the proper perception of its form when listening. When listeners are so involved, they become like agents willfully pursuing the musical goals established by the piece, and the work becomes like a world in which these agents are engaged. This illusion is made more real to the degree that the listeners' cognitive capacities are involved as well in grasping the unfolding musical forms. Experiencing the more common human emotions adds further to their full immersion in the world of the work, and it makes this world more of a human world, and so often more absorbing as well. If this complete absorption in the world of a work, involving to the fullest the occupation of our cognitive and affective capacities, and making the experience of each element of the work richer in relating it to others, explains the value of many artworks for us, then it also explains the contribution to that value of those features of works that engage our emotions.

It explains also the value of negative emotions in the context of art, which is inexplicable in other terms when considered in isolation from other sources of value and from their contribution to the overall value of works. Full absorption in the worlds of artworks, which implies escape from the real world (and possibly subsequent reflection on it), can be intensely satisfying even when particular aspects of it in isolation are not. Negative emotions parallel on the affective side the cognitive challenge that many works present. Such challenges help to prompt our full engagement in the works that present them. The fact that musical works can condense many emotional states and changes into a much smaller time frame than occurs in real life, which, we noted above, makes music an inaccurate map of emotional life, also makes the experience of musical passages more intense and intensely significant.

To say that our involvement in such intense experience is its own reward, and that the value of emotion properties in music lies in their contribution to this experience, is compatible with acknowledgment that there can be great works of music that do not arouse anything like ordinary emotions. Many string quartets of Haydn, for example, engage us through their perfectly crafted forms, sensuous beauty, and internal affects without being naturally categorized in ordinary emotion terms. And there are also pieces naturally categorized as sad or happy that are not particularly good pieces. This is once more compatible with the fact that emotional expression can add to the value of many pieces, even be essential to it, by being an essential part of our full involvement with those works.

We have noted a variety of base properties that function in different ways as means of expression in music. In literature and painting, the more standardly representational arts, expression is more typically tied to representations, to specific content that can be characterized in nonexpressive terms as well. Literary works, of course, can simply describe emotional states directly or, slightly more indirectly, describe the behavior of persons in those states or the ways things appear to persons in those states. Related to the last method but yet more subtle, literary passages can be expressed in a style that reflects a narrator's frame of mind, for example, agitated or numb. Literature can evoke emotions by describing those states of affairs that would evoke them in real life. Which of these various methods is called expression as well as description is not settled by current usage. Expression of emotion in painting can be similarly related to representation in a variety of ways. Paintings can depict the facial expressions or demeanors of persons in the grip of emotions, or they can depict scenes that look the way they do to such persons or that seem to fit their moods. Various color combinations can evoke affective reactions, as can brush strokes or delineations of forms (e.g., sharply angular versus gently curving) that seem to reflect states of mind of the artists who produced them. Perhaps none of this is as philosophically controversial as the nature and value of representation itself in painting, the topic to which we now turn.

Representation

Representation in music is minimal and shades into expression. Representation in literature is ubiquitous and reduces to reference and description, which are very large and not predominantly aesthetic topics.[19] Aesthetic controversy centers on pictorial representation or depiction. This section will address once more both the nature of such representation as a base property and why it is a basis for aesthetic value and evaluation. The first questions are: What makes a dab of paint a representation? and What is the criterion for its representing x rather than y? From the earliest discussions of these questions, they have been linked to the question of the aesthetic value of depiction.

Plato gave birth to aesthetics when he claimed that a painting imitates (aims to reproduce) the appearance of an object.[20] This claim both suggests a criterion of pictorial representation and, for Plato, makes its value problematic. Before addressing the problem of value, we may spell out the criterion, first by adding that a painting succeeds in representing its intended object when the aim in question succeeds. The proposed criterion can be specified in contemporary terms as follows:

A painting P represents (depicts) an object O = (1) its artist intends by marking P's surface to create visual experience that resembles the experience of O; (2) when P is seen in normal conditions, the experience does resemble that of O; and (3) because of 2, O can be seen in P and the artist's intention is recoverable from the experience, sometimes together with supplementary information.

As so interpreted and supplemented, I believe the criterion stands up, despite much criticism in the more recent literature of the centrality of the notion of resemblance here.

It is easy to show that resemblance is not sufficient for representation and that even resemblance plus representation (in a broad sense) do not add up to depiction or pictorial representation. I borrow freely from Nelson Goodman's well-known examples: Twins resemble but do not represent each other; prints of a painting resemble the painting more than the painting resembles what it represents; and a sample of a fabric resembles *and* represents (in the broad sense) the fabric, but it does not depict it (it is not a pictorial representation). Furthermore, resemblance is a reflexive and symmetrical relation; representation is neither.[21] Another example: The depiction of a dog in Velázquez's *Las Meninas* represents a particular dog, the one belonging to that royal family, but it resembles many other similar dogs.

The proposed criterion does not hold resemblance to be sufficient; it must be combined with a particular intention and causal process. Intention to represent, of course, is not sufficient either, even if followed by marking of a flat surface. A child's intending a dab of paint to represent his mommy does not make it a depiction of his mommy unless others are able to see his mommy in the picture. An intention to represent something can be successful or unsuccessful, and thus representation depends on more than intention. Intention is, however, necessary. Accidental likenesses, as in shapes in clouds, are not representations. Artists' intentions can also pick out what is represented from among the possibilities, for example, a specific dog in *Las Meninas* or a particular bowl of fruit as opposed to kinds of dogs or fruit. Although intention is necessary for representation, the latter is a transparent and not intentionally opaque concept. If a student copies a painting of Washington crossing the Delaware, then she depicts a former president, although she may not intend to do the latter (aiming to represent that figure in the painting but not knowing that he is President Washington).

The causal process mentioned is that of marking a surface. No causal relation to object is mentioned. Although that causal relation does seem crucial for determining the objects of percepts and photographs, paintings are different in this respect. The causal relation between a still life and the bowl of fruit it represents (if, indeed, it represents a particular real bowl of fruit) is most like the relation of a painting of a Biblical figure to its real-life model (if it had one), not to the Biblical character. And yet the latter painting is a depiction of that character and not of its model. Thus there is no particular causal relation to object that determines what a picture represents (think of the differences in this regard between a portrait, a depiction of a Biblical figure via a model, and a representation of a mythical beast).

By contrast, a causal relation between the marking of the surface and the intention of the artist is necessary, as noted. What should we say of a case in which an artist intends and believes that she is representing a street scene on Fifth Avenue when she is actually sitting on Madison Avenue, painting the scene before her? Her painting, we would say, is a picture of Madison Avenue. Is this a case where the causal relation to object overrides the artist's intention? No, because the artist also intends to represent the scene before her, only verbally misdescribing it to herself. The causal relation to the artist or her intention remains more important than that to the represented object, unlike the case of a photograph. The resulting process of marking the canvas, the causal context of the painting's production that is included in the criterion, rules out Goodman's example of a fabric sample (which he uses for a different purpose) as a counterexample. Although the fabric sample is intended to represent the fabric it resembles exactly, it is not a depiction because it is not produced by marking a canvas in an appropriate way.

The example of the painting of the Biblical figure seems problematic for the claim that resemblance is necessary for depiction. It seems to show not only that resemblance (of painting to model) is not sufficient for pictorial representation but also that it (resemblance of painting to Biblical character) is not necessary either. Here intention plus convention (conventional ways of representing the character) seem to suffice. But, in response, the case still seems relevantly different from another sort of case in which intention and convention suffice for a different sort of representation in a painting. I have in mind a symbolic reference that is not a depiction of what it symbolically represents, for example, a symbolization of Christ as a lamb. What makes this not a depiction of Christ, even though it is a pictorial representation of him of a different kind (and a depiction of a lamb), seems to be the lack of some kind of resemblance. But what kind? In the case of literal depiction of a Biblical figure, the figure in the painting resembles the artist's image of the person, based perhaps on descriptions and on other historical evidence including art objects from the period. Similar remarks apply to the case of depicting mythical characters, except that here we confront the artist's image of how a character would have looked if he had been real. If resemblance is what distinguishes the depictive from the nondepictive reference in these examples, then it seems again to be necessary for depiction.

In these unusual cases of Biblical and mythological figures, recovering the artist's intention from the resemblance of one's experience of her painting to her image of the object (instead of to experience of the object) might require knowledge of conventions (conventional ways of representing the figures). This would be included in the analysis under supplementary information, which might also include titles of paintings. This role for convention is both subordinate and unusual, in sharp contrast to Goodman's account. In rejecting resemblance as relevant, Goodman described pictorial representation as a conventional symbolic system akin to language in its referential aspects but differing in the formal structure of its symbols. We need not survey his interesting list of differences. It is more important to note that pictorial representation is, despite his points, very little like a conventional language.

To recognize and interpret a painting as representational, we do not need to know semantic rules to relate its discrete parts to objects in the world or syntactic rules for putting those parts together. My own son's first word was "baby," uttered in his first year not in the presence of another infant but when he saw a diaper box in a supermarket with a picture (not a photograph) of a baby on it. Although he needed to learn the conventional meaning of the word to accomplish this feat, I do not believe that he had previously learned in a similar way how to interpret a picture of that sort. He was able to do so simply in virtue of his ability to recognize a baby's face. This was a matter of assimilating perceptual experiences, not associating a symbol with its object via learned convention. If depiction were mainly a matter of convention, then the picture of the baby might just as easily have depicted a giraffe, and my son's feat would have been impossible at that stage of his development.

Flint Schier has proposed a criterion of pictorial representation based on its not being conventional. Roughly, according to him, something is a picture of O if we can naturally interpret it visually as O, if this interpretation depends only on our ability to recognize O.[22] Unlike our Platonic criterion, this one eschews appeal to resemblance. But we may question whether it is most deeply explanatory of the nature of base properties for pictorial representations. First, the recognitional capacity that is triggered by a picture of O in this account can be explained, it seems, by appeal to the resemblance between the experiences of seeing the picture and of seeing O.[23] Thus the deeper account appeals to this relation instead of to the recognitional capacity and interpretive ability the relation explains. Second, the criterion of "natural generativity" breaks down exactly where the usually crucial sort of resemblance between appearance of picture and appearance of object does not suffice for pictorial representation. As noted, a picture may represent a Biblical figure even though it resembles its contemporary model more. But then in this case our ability to recognize the Biblical figure in the closest possible world in which we encountered him would not suffice to interpret the painting as a picture of him. The failure of Schier's criterion here results from the lack of requisite likeness between representation and object and from the fact that resemblance must be supplemented by other information. This indicates not only that the criterion fails to be universal but also that it depends on the more fundamental relation.

Other current authors as well have proposed criteria for depiction of an object that avoid appeal to resemblance. One that is included in our analysis is that we must be able to see an object in a painting for it to be a depiction of that object.[24] This condition is necessary but once more not sufficient. A person might be able to form visual images on blank surfaces without thereby turning those surfaces into representations. There must be some features on the surface that explain why normal viewers see the object represented in it for it to be a representation of that object. When such features do explain what we see in a painted surface, they point once more to our deeper or more illuminating criterion.

Similar remarks apply to Kendall Walton's claim that a painting is a depiction if it prescribes us to imagine that our experience of looking at it is visual experience of some real object. According to Walton it depicts a particular object if it is fictional that one's looking at the painting is one's looking at the object, if one is to imagine this of one's visual experience.[25] If we do use pictures in the sorts of imaginative games that Walton describes (more on this below), and if the pictures naturally facilitate our doing so, this is again because of certain relations the pictures bear to their represented objects. It is because the experience of looking at them is like the experience of looking at their objects that we might be tempted to play such games in which the pictures function as props for imagination.

Goodman believes that resemblance is empty as a necessary condition for depiction, since there are countless ways in which all objects both do and do not resemble each other. This point, however, does not show that there are no necessary resemblances involved in depiction; it only calls upon us to specify what sorts of resemblances are relevant or necessary. Just as we cannot count objects or kinds of objects without some specification of what kinds of objects are at issue, so we cannot measure or even speak of resemblance *tout court* without relevant respects being specified or understood. In the case of pictorial representation relevant resemblances will relate only to visual appearance. They are those required to recover the intention of the artist and to see the represented object in the painting. Similarity of shape in the visual field is usually crucial but not always so.[26] A child's depiction of a leaf may depend more for its success on its bright green color, for example.[27]

Our account emphasizes resemblance more than do Goodman, Schier, or Walton, and it emphasizes convention less than they do. We might, following Schier, speak of a fundamental general convention that sufficient resemblance will be taken by an audience to indicate an intention on the part of an artist to represent the object of which the picture is a likeness.[28] But such a convention is not needed, since this intention would naturally be inferred as the best explanation for the likeness anyway. We might, following Walton, take some less general conventions particular to painting to affect depiction. We might take it as conventional that the lack of resemblance between two and three spatial dimensions is irrelevant or that, for example, horses depicted with their legs extended off the ground are not represented as frozen in space but as galloping. But since we never perceive horses frozen in space, we need no convention to know that they would not be represented that way (without many other clues in the picture). And since the lack of literal resemblance to a third dimension or to movement derive directly from limitations of the medium, they can again be known to be irrelevant without the need for conventions to tell us so. I conclude that, aside from the above-noted conventional ways of representing certain figures, convention has little to do with criteria for depiction. This is not to deny that different styles of painting have different conventions for ways of representing, only to say that these have little effect on what is represented or, more precisely, on how we determine what is represented.

Representation is determined by a combination of intention, causal context of production, and resemblance of experience of picture to that of object in relevant respects, sometimes supplemented by convention. Once more we find a complex base property, partially captured by simpler earlier analyses. As a definition, our account may sound circular, since the object represented is mentioned in it. But there is no problematic circularity. The account specifies which object is represented by describing it as the one that the artist successfully intends the experience of the picture to resemble. It is important to emphasize that the criterion refers to resemblances among visual experiences and not between object and representation themselves. These are importantly different because visual cues must be different in a flat and stationary, as opposed to an ordinary three-dimensional, array. This fact explains the truth of Ernst Gombrich's central claim that an artist cannot simply copy nature but must instead discover and correct artistic schemas to which visual appearance can be assimilated to produce a lifelike effect.[29] But since resemblance of this sort too comes in degrees, being a successful representation falls in a scale somewhere between failure and perfect realism or true-to-lifeness.

Of course, 'realism' in painting, as in other arts, has many senses. One is primarily social: A work of art that is realistic in this sense shows life as it really is or was, often its seamier or more mundane side. Or a picture captures the predominant values of a time or place. Another sense closer to the one we are after has to do with the richness of detail in a work. A painting that represents an object always represents it as having certain properties. It does this either by having or appearing to have the properties, such as various col-

ors (resembling the object in these very respects), or by representing the properties (by other resemblances), as in the case of depicting a horse as galloping. Part of being true-to-life in the sense relevant here lies in the quantity or richness of the visual properties that
the objects are depicted as having. The more important part lies in
the represented objects, if they are real objects, having the properties they are depicted as having. Or realism consists in the probability of objects of the kind represented, if they are not particular real
objects, having the properties they are represented as having.

Since the relevant resemblances relate visual properties, what
matters in judging the degree of realism in a picture is that the
painted surface trigger visual responses or experiences similar to
those caused by the array of objects depicted. This similarity of
overall perceptual response does not depend on the appearances or
absolute properties of isolable parts of the array, whether on canvas
or in real space. Instead, relations within the reflected light from the
two-dimensional surface must trigger similar responses to those set
off by relations within the reflected light from a three-dimensional
scene. Apparent colors are relational in this sense, not to be identified with isolated colored patches as projected in the retina. When it
comes to shapes and sizes, a rough approximation to true-to-life
appearance results from the application of geometrical optics. This
application captures the occlusion shapes and sizes of objects
through such painterly devices as foreshortening and perspective
diminution.[30] The approximation to realism from this projection
onto the flat surface is not perfect, in part because some cues for the
normal size and shape constancies derive from movement within a
three-dimensional array and from binocular depth disparities, and
these cannot simply be reproduced on a painted surface.

But this does not imply that realistic perspective, or realistic appearance in a painting more broadly, is a matter of learned convention or of what we are used to seeing and interpreting on painted
surfaces. If realism were conventional in this way, then Picassos
would look more lifelike to most of us than works of the High
Renaissance. But what we are most used to seeing and interpreting
in modern painting still looks flat and distorted to us. (That it looks
this way is, of course, necessary to its expressive effects, formal
structures, and implicit historical commentaries.) That Renaissance
paintings look more lifelike is explained by the closer resemblance
between our experience of them and our visual experience of real

scenes. This, in turn, is explained by the discovery in that period of
those relations among elements or spatial parts on painted surfaces
that approximate in visual effects relations functioning as cues
within ordinary reflected light. Such resemblances and the complex
relations that underlie them also explain the ease with which we can
see represented objects in paintings. These then are the resemblances relevant to pictorial representation and, beyond the threshold of seeing-in necessary for minimal depiction, relevant to realistic representation as well. When we combine these with the
requisite intentions and causal contexts, we have those complex
base properties that constitute a major source of value in much of
visual art.

But if resemblance is the main ingredient in depiction, then it becomes puzzling, as it did to Plato, why representations of this sort
should have value, aesthetic or otherwise. More precisely, he
wanted to know why a mere imitation of an object or apprehension
of such an imitation should possess any value not possessed by the
original or by the perception or direct knowledge of it. Three kinds
of answers were later typically proposed. The first emphasizes what
a picture can reveal about its object that may not be revealed in perceiving the object itself; the second points to the way that paintings
are supposed to train or alter our vision of objects and scenes in the
real world; and the third appeals to the exercise of imagination that
pictorial representation affords or occasions. I shall comment
briefly on each of these answers, concluding that all are problematic
if taken to indicate a general source of artistic value that typically
contributes to the greatness of great representational paintings.

The plausibility of the first answer, which locates the value of
representation in the knowledge it provides of its objects, derives
mainly from the genre of portraiture and secondarily from history
paintings, which depict significant or climactic moments from religious, mythological, or political narratives. A portrait can answer
Plato's question if it succeeds in revealing important facets of its
subject's personality or, better yet, the key to the subject's personal
identity when such are not ordinarily revealed in a person's physical appearance. Portrait artists have often sought to depict character
or identity in this way, but we can question whether success in this
regard is really even possible. Is there such a core to an individual's
psyche? And if so, can it be revealed in any physical appearance or
representation? There are such things as nasty looks, for example
(although such are rarely intentionally represented in portraits),

and there are certain semiconventional ways (based originally on mistaken theories) of representing high intelligence, for example, with a broad forehead. Beyond that, we can sometimes read emotions and perhaps such traits as intensity or resignation from people's faces and demeanors, whether real or represented. But none of this takes us very far in capturing or apprehending an individual's unique psychic identity. More often than not expressions and overall appearances in portraits, even many great ones, seem artificial and posed, revealing mainly their subjects' social status and the images they want to project for posterity if the artists choose to cooperate in this projection.

There are, it is true, some portraits that seem to dig deeper. We see Picasso's famous depiction of Gertrude Stein and seem to be confronted by her acuity, solidity, and forcefulness. But if we did not have independent knowledge of her, and if she were portrayed in a different context, her look could be that of an ignorant peasant. Plato's problem with representational art was not simply that it fails to reflect or provide genuine knowledge of its objects but also that it tempts us to substitute its appearance for genuine knowledge by appealing to our senses and emotions rather than to our intellects, as do philosophy and science. The illusion of knowing people from their portraits supplies the best ground for this Platonic worry.

This is not to say that portraits do not have special virtues among painting genres, among them the aforementioned revelation of the social ideals, values, and pretensions of different times and places. They provide seeming personal contact with various social types and also with famous personalities who may become identified as much with their portraits as with their deeds and descriptions. But, as in the case of "bringing to life" through paintings well-known episodes from narratives of various kinds, the value here lies more in the exercise of imagination, in the imaginative personal contact with figures known only more abstractly, than in any genuine knowledge gained of the objects or subjects depicted. Other values endemic to portraiture are more clearly aesthetic and even less epistemic. The relations revealed among individuals portrayed in group portraits, for example, help to determine formal structures on different levels of the works that help to constitute satisfying aesthetic experiences of them.

At the opposite extreme in its lack of pretense of providing knowledge, insight, or deep truth about its subject matter is the genre of still life. There are minor exceptions here. Some seventeenth-century Dutch flower paintings depict species that were then exotic in Europe, and at least some of their value was thought to derive from the value of their objects being seen and known for the first time. But for the most part still life artists eschewed depiction of those objects of which we might naturally seek more knowledge. Their paintings tell us nothing (directly) about the human psyche or about great or important events (in fact nothing happens in them).[31] Although they may reveal indirectly something of the values of the artist or of the culture in which they are embedded (for example, by representing simple domestic scenes or great material abundance), they provide little knowledge not readily available elsewhere of fruits or flowers or even of vases and tables. That their value does not lie in such knowledge suffices to show that this first sort of answer to Plato's question cannot be generalized across representational paintings.

The genre of still life instead suggests the second sort of answer—that what is valuable here is the effect of such paintings on the ways that we see. Many of these paintings can be interpreted as inviting our visual attention to the sensuous qualities of objects that we normally overlook or merely scan in our ordinary practical pursuits. The sharpness of focus that is often evenly distributed across the entire painted surface or directed at otherwise insignificant qualities makes it plausible that many still lifes exemplify or refer to the properties of the represented objects they display,[32] intentionally calling our attention to qualities we usually miss, to the aesthetic impoverishment of our ordinary experience. According to Nelson Goodman, a primary function of art is to retrain our vision in this way to see the world in new and aesthetically more satisfying ways.[33] When the painting is representational, this thesis is perhaps most plausible in the genre of still life.

But Goodman's thesis here is closely connected to his claim, evaluated earlier, that representation is mainly conventional. One of the grounds on which he attacks the resemblance criterion is his belief that we encounter objects in perception only through active construals or interpretations,[34] so that there is no way to say that a painting resembles an object as it is in itself or as we always perceive it. The new claim also presupposes a plasticity in our perceptual systems that must be questioned. Following the dominant psychology of the time, Goodman's claims exaggerate the relativity of visual perception to the subject's cognitive and affective input. This exaggeration was typical of reports of experiments in the psychology of perception in the 1950s and 1960s. These experiments typically employed very abnormal viewing conditions and times, in which objects could barely be recognized, to demonstrate such relativity under the highly questionable assumption that generalizations could be drawn from perceptual guesses in such conditions.[35]

Does looking at paintings or listening to music typically alter the way we look and see, listen and hear, outside the context of appreciating art? Speaking for myself in the case of music, ordinary noises sound only worse to me by comparison after hearing a symphony. And I find no evidence for Goodman's claim that listening to music can alter our perceptions of rhythms and patterns in phenomena that are not sonic.[36] In the case of painting, seeing a Cézanne still life might encourage us, if we have the time, to appreciate the colors of some ripe peaches before eating them, although we will probably also note with disapproval the disorder of their array on our table and the irregularity of their shapes in comparison with the represented shapes in the Cézanne. Seeing patterns and colors in paintings can alter the ways we see patterns in real visual arrays if we make the deliberate effort to seek similar patterns there, but that it typically has such effects is far more dubious. In any case, abstract patterns can be just as effective in this regard as representational ones, so that representation would have no special value here.

In general, the ways visual fields appear *can* radically alter, especially in cases where systematic distortions have been introduced and then, over time, tend to correct, but seemingly always in response to and at the service of actions or behavior involving the other sense modalities.[37] Cognitive grasp alone is insufficient for such effects, as is evident from the persistence of the standard visual illusions despite full understanding of their nature. The general subordination of the visual system to the aims of practical behavior is predictably hard wired through biological evolution, to the detriment of any major effects on that system from viewing art and to any thesis that locates the value of representational art there. It is more likely that looking at art alters the ways we look at and see subsequent art, where practical motivations are minimal and we use vision without behaving in ways that involve the other sense modalities directly. Such effects do not support the second kind of answer to Plato.

The third type of answer is best typified by Kendall Walton's theory of representation. According to him, all representations function as props in games of make-believe. By generating fictional truths within prescribed games, they require us to imagine in common certain things, and in the case of paintings, to imagine them visually. When we look at a landscape painting, for example, we are to imagine seeing that rural scene. Participants in these games expand upon the fictional worlds of artworks by including themselves in the worlds of their games, by imagining the worlds of the works from the inside, as if they were in them. The value of artistic representations on this account lies in the ways they serve as aids to coordinated imagination, and hence it derives directly from the value of exercising imagination itself. In addition to the enjoyment involved in this exercise, one can broaden one's horizons by engaging in these games. In complex games of fiction, one can learn responses to new types of situations, learn about oneself and how one responds to different situations, and learn to empathize with others.[38] The representational props help less imaginative persons share in the imaginative lives of those more creative and allows them to communicate their imaginative experiences to each other by reference to the artworks. Thus games of make-believe facilitated by these props broaden the scope of imaginative life and allow participants in the games to share their imaginary worlds.

In evaluating this proposal, it seems obvious that it fits the context of literary representation more comfortably than that of painting.[39] Imaginatively identifying with characters in novels can benefit readers in the ways the theory indicates: They can try out unfamiliar roles and character traits, empathize with the characters and sympathize with their plights, hence vicariously expanding their emotional repertoires and moral capacities. But none of this applies to anything like the same degree to viewing visual artworks, at least not in my experience. This is not to deny that imagination can be involved in the appreciation of representational painting. It is more typically involved at a basic, unreflective, and perhaps subconscious level in filling out objects and scenes based on sometimes rather meager cues on the painted surfaces. At a higher level we may sometimes engage in primitive Walton-type games with paintings, as when we seem to make personal contact with the subject of a portrait. But whereas some paintings encourage this sort of thing by implicating the viewer in the relations they represent, others discourage it. Some still lifes, for example, Lubin Baugin's *Dessert with Wafers* at the Louvre, seem to invite reaching out and taking the represented food from the table; others, such as most of Cézanne's still lifes, emphasize formal structure to the extent that any imagined action on the viewer's part would destroy the aesthetic point of the array. Likewise, central characters in some portraits of Manet, for example, seem to avert their gazes from the viewer, who is therefore implicated in the worlds of the paintings, whereas others, such as Parmigianino's self-portrait, Van Eyck's *Giovanni Arnolfini and His Bride,* and *Las Meninas,* depict mirror reflections that exclude the viewer from any imagined space within their represented worlds.

Paintings may discourage Walton-type imaginative games in more subtle ways as well. Walton recognizes that such games are most easily played with the most true-to-life representations (in fact, as we saw above, he tries to develop this point into an explanatory account of realism). It is perhaps partly for this very reason that so many artists, beginning with Tintoretto, El Greco, and other mannerists at a time soon after the means to truly realistic representation had been discovered and perfected, deliberately violate the norms of true-to-life perspective and depiction in general. To be sure, they do so for expressive and formal effects but also because works in which only one source of aesthetic value completely dominates often fail to strike us as great works. Works of exquisite form but without interesting content or expressiveness are apt to strike us as cold and lifeless. Highly expressive works without coherent form, content, or historical importance often seem strident, raucous, or lacking in subtlety. Most to the point here, realistic representation alone may seem a mere technical achievement without much artistic value; paintings that achieve only realism often seem superficial or sentimental, despite their easy use in Walton-type games. In fact, vivid and realistic representation especially, with its immediate appeal to imagination, constitutes a common threat to the unsophisticated viewer's perception of other aesthetically significant aspects of artworks. When such viewers succumb to its lure and surrender to imaginative reveries, even those "authorized" by the paintings' representational content, their cognitive faculties will not be fully engaged.

In viewing a painting, affect should be guided by apprehension of form instead of floating free on mere association, and imagination should be controlled by an understanding of how representational and symbolic content are achieved through formal and expressive means. Only in this way is the Kantian ideal of a harmony between imagination and understanding realized (whether we are thinking of his technical sense of 'imagination' or Walton's more usual sense). And only in this way can viewers meet Dewey's requirement that their subjective activities harmonize with their receptions of the structures of artworks. Viewing in accord with Walton's theory seems to allow active imagination to dominate over receptive cognition (where cognition includes not simply recognition of what is represented but also appreciation of formal relations and symbolic content), forfeiting that full aesthetic experience that both Kant and Dewey celebrate.

I am suggesting that, as in the case of expression, understanding the aesthetic value of representation and the base properties that account for it requires us to note the ways that these base properties interact with the other sources of aesthetic value so as to prompt the interaction of our perceptual, cognitive, and affective capacities in appreciating the artworks that contain them. Only in this way can we understand the *aesthetic* value of representation, which Walton's theory does not explain. For him, paintings and other representations function for adults much as do toys in games for children. But toys acquire no aesthetic value from functioning as props in games of make-believe, and neither do illustrations in books of fiction, which of all pictorial representations come closest to serving just the function that Walton describes. To appreciate the value of representation within pictorial art we must note how from the objective side it serves as a means of expression and source of symbolic content and, only slightly less obviously, how it contributes to form. And we must appreciate from the subjective side how it creates and enriches perceptual, cognitive, and affective content.

It is easy to provide illustrations of the relation of pictorial representation to other sources of value in paintings. We can begin at the bottom, with pure sensuous beauty. It appears at first that this source of pleasure in art is divorced from others and especially from representational content. But this is not always so. The beauty of the flesh tones in a Titian or Renoir is greatly enhanced by their being *flesh* tones, colors of human skin often reflecting intense vitality or eroticism. Expressive properties of paintings are more typically associated with representational content. These properties do not, of course, always rely on depiction (or we could not fathom the abstract expressionist movement). We noted above that colors, brush strokes, and formal elements can be expressive in themselves. But despite the unmitigated effusiveness of some critics in describing the expressiveness of certain abstract works, there can be little doubt that masterful representations communicate affect to most viewers more powerfully. This is because they can depict those subject matters with which we are most naturally concerned: facial expressions, natural or domestic scenes, and so on.

The contribution of representation to form should be only slightly less obvious. Although formalists such as Clive Bell hold depiction to be at best irrelevant and at worst a hindrance to the appreciation of form, and although I admitted above that exclusive attention to what is represented can block full aesthetic appreciation on the part of naive audiences, depiction can generate levels of formal structure unavailable to the purely abstract artist. First, representations group formal elements—lines, shapes, colors—into natural larger units (objects) so that formal relations may then emerge on a higher level (among objects and groups of them), creating a hierarchy of material forms. Second, representation adds new elements and dimensions to the basic lines and shapes in the apparent physical space of paintings: the third spatial dimension (to a greater degree than in fully abstract works), illumination, texture, weight, and movement. These elements greatly enrich the possibilities for formal relations (tensions, balances, and so on) within that space. Third, it introduces nonphysical elements into its represented scenes: human characters with their assortment of traits, actions, social settings. These can be organized into formal structures as well. Here representation fully creates the elements it relates, as in novels, although the relations among them—parallels, tensions, oppositions, harmonies—will not be as complex as in novels unless the paintings represent complex stories. Finally, the represented physical forms connect to the nonphysical so as to create higher-level formal relations. Character and action can fit physical setting, for example, or they can contrast ironically, as in Brueghel's representation of the Icarus legend.[40]

The importance of representation to formal structure is perfectly clear from the way that many almost abstract cubist works retain recognizable objects such as guitars and violins that unify diverse spatial planes so that our visual systems can make sense of otherwise incomprehensible spaces. Another good example referred to earlier (among the countless ones that might be mentioned here) of

FIGURE 3.1   James Abbott McNeill Whistler, *Arrangement in Grey and Black No. 1: The Artist's Mother*, canvas, 56 × 64", Musée d'Orsay, Paris.

the interaction of represented nonphysical and physical structures is Whistler's portrait of his mother (which comes to mind again because its title, *Arrangement in Grey and Black*, makes clear that the artist intended to emphasize this relation). (See Figure 3.1.) As mentioned in the earlier reference, we perhaps notice first here the relations among the nonphysical represented traits—the quiet repose and dignity and perhaps resignation in the facial expression and pose of the subject and the way that this expression matches the action (or total lack of it) and quiet setting of the painting. Then we see how, like so many fine works, this one derives it subtle power of expression from the way this structure emerges from and reinforces the physical elements and forms in the work: the gently downward sloping central line, the stable balance of object forms on the canvas, and especially the blend of muted colors, with delicate highlights to prevent visual boredom and emphasize expressive forms such as the hands. The character represented here is captured and echoed in the understated formal elements and relations, a typical higher-order relation that is, of course, impossible without representation.

Such interactions between representation and other sources of value in artworks provide an explanation of its primary aesthetic value alternative to the ones considered above. The hyperclarity of many still lifes, for example, can be interpreted not as a means to retrain vision but as a way to achieve a heightened sensuous effect and sense of form. Objects are chosen here not for the knowledge we can gain of them but as higher-order formal elements that can engage our perceptual interest purely for its own sake. Our cognitive faculty or understanding is involved in grasping how formal elements in the paint create content, how represented content generates formal structure on a higher level, and how the total work relates to others in the tradition. The choice of objects without special interest or value other than aesthetic makes it easier to answer Plato's question here. In fully exercising our mental capacities, the representational artwork here clearly exceeds in value the objects represented, and Plato's challenge is met. Representation does not merely provide copies of objects that are of less use than the originals; it helps to create imaginary worlds in which we lose our ordinary selves. We do so not primarily by imagining ourselves in the represented scenes (as in Walton's account) but by becoming involved in uniquely aesthetic ways. Once more it is in terms of its contribution to this whole experience that we are to understand this source of aesthetic value and the value of the base properties that underlie it.

That the provision of such experience is what many great works have in common is evidenced also by the prevalence in both painting and literature of another kind of representation that creates yet another level of content: symbolic content. A symbol in this sense is a representation of something concrete that resists full interpretation in strictly literal terms. The symbolic object appears superficially to be out of place or mysteriously emphasized or repeated. The best explanation for its otherwise puzzling place in the work requires us to note the properties it has in common with other usually more abstract objects or ideas that figure prominently in the broad meaning or theme of the work. The symbol thus creates a metaphorical connection from the concrete to the more abstract. (Many metaphors run in the opposite direction.) Often there is also a transference of affect from the emotionally laden abstract idea or object to the symbol and hence to the expressive effect of the work that contains it.

The general value of symbols as such lies in the heightened significance, the condensation or intensification of the experience of the artworks that contain them, and in the satisfaction that grasping that significance affords. A symbol condenses the import of an emotionally charged abstract idea into a concrete image, and interpreting that image presents a challenge to the understanding whose solution is pleasurable in the way that solving any puzzle is. The discovery of latent symbolic content is in this respect like the perceptual grasp of complex form, which renders previously disconnected space and time intelligible. On a higher level of cognitive functioning the symbol as a focal point may tie together disparate parts of a work under a common theme. Its multifaceted significance, which seems to overflow the concrete image into which it is condensed, unites perception, cognition, and affect into a more intensely meaningful experience. Yet again at this level where the concrete and abstract merge, the value of representation, like that of expression, can be found in its contribution, along with the other sources of aesthetic value, to this experience.

Form

Form is the basest (nonevaluative sense) of the base properties, the type of property on which most other aesthetic properties ultimately depend. We saw that representation and expression do not depend only on formal properties of works—intentions, historical contexts, conventions, and style figure in their base properties as well. But these, we might say, help to determine how best to interpret the formal properties in expressive and representational terms so that the formal relations remain the basis on which these other evaluatively crucial properties depend. If this is the formalists' claim, they are right. If they tell us in addition to attend only to formal properties of works, they are wrong, for then we will miss much of aesthetic value, including, as we saw in the previous section, much of the higher-level formal structure of works.

There is no deep analytical problem in specifying what form in artworks is. In contrast to the cases of expression and representation, problems in analysis here come only in specifying the complex forms of particular works, how all their significant elements relate to each other on different levels. As just suggested, the unproblematic definition is that form consists in relations among elements of works, relations constituting some intelligible order of these elements. Form relates units on various levels into larger groups or wholes that can be grasped in the course of experiencing a work. Thus, to specify a work's form, one must specify the units on each level of consideration and the sorts of relations that combine them into larger structures that lend coherence to or guide one's perception or experience of the work. Relations or structures on one level become elements on the next until we arrive at a set of relations among broad sections that make up the whole work.

Before I provide examples, I will make one further preliminary point. I said that aesthetic form can be grasped in the course of experiencing a work of art, but much of what is called structure on the largest scale, especially in music, is not explicitly experienced as such by any but the most highly trained listeners, and by them only when listening in an analytic frame of mind. It is difficult not to identify this broad structure of a piece or movement with aesthetic form. To continue to do so in light of this fact of common musical experience, we can take one of two analytic routes. We can either define form in terms of relations experienced as such by ideal listeners (with ideally coherent and detailed or differentiated experience of a work) or we can define form in terms of relations that affect or inform the ways that their parts or relata are perceived, relations that could in principle but need not be perceived as such within the work. A theme repeated or reinterpreted in a recapitulation section of a sonata movement is normally heard differently from the way it was heard for the first time in the exposition, as right or familiar even if not as repeated. The large structure affects the aesthetic properties heard within the smaller forms, those that are normally experienced as such. In this way the broadest forms within complex works remain aesthetically relevant.

In modern orchestral music, elements consist first of tones, which are themselves complex in consisting of experientially inseparable pitches, durations, and instrument colors. Tones can be but ordinarily are not heard as individual elements. What are so heard are melodic motifs, phrases, and themes (which typically consist of antecedent and consequent phrases). Themes are not simply melodic but are rhythmical as well, and they are combined with tempi, dynamics, orchestration, and harmonies. We can trace progressions in sections of pieces in all these musical elements. In tonal music certain progressions create more or less closed forms, which, depending on degree of closure, create elements for the next-highest level of hierarchical structure in a movement or piece. Generally, repetitions and variations of closed forms (especially repetition after contrast) create higher-level structures with their own degree of completeness.

Harmonically, for example, movement from a dominant chord or key back to the tonic with a full cadence constitutes complete closure. Melodically, rising or oscillating patterns call for returns; gaps call for fills. Rhythmically, accents after nonaccented beats appear more closed. Conversely, evenly accented tones, regularly rising melodic patterns, constant variation or transformation, and tonal progression from tonic or subdominant to dominant or relative minor are unstable or open, pointing the listener ahead in expectation of further development and ultimate resolution. Progressions within these different parameters may be congruent or divergent, again contributing to degree of closure.[41] Congruent progression toward a climax, for example, might involve accelerating tempo, increasing volume, fuller orchestration, and harmonic movement toward a cadence. Musical themes may be repeated (with the same or different harmonic accompaniments and tempi), varied, contrasted, fragmented and developed, combined, or played in counterpoint. These thematic (melodic and rhythmic) changes, together with harmonic progressions and cadences and orchestral texture, mark off sections of movements for the listener.

The same sorts of structures, although usually not as complex or formally developed, exist in the visual and literary arts, where, of course, the elements are different. In painting, elements include lines, colors, shapes, sizes, lighting, represented objects, movements, masses, groups of objects, perspectives. Again, various elements within this diverse but nonexhaustive set may be thematized in a given painting, that is, repeated, varied, developed, contrasted, and so on, creating higher-order relations such as balance, proportion, symmetry, or tension. Recall also those nonphysical higher-order elements mentioned in the section on representation. The latter are the basic elements of literature as well, where we may find significant formal relations among characters and their traits, events, episodes, settings, points of view, and so on. As a temporal form akin to music, literary works often contain dramatic conflict and resolution at the heart of their large-scale formal structures.

One of the most complex, successful, and enduring formal frameworks in the arts is the sonata-allegro form that is typical of first movements in symphonies in the classical style. In approaching the question of value in this section, we may use this structure for purposes of further illustration. Although there is considerable flexibility and variation in practice, certain features of this form are typical. Movements employing this framework contain three thematically and harmonically related sections that combine conflict and drama with balance and symmetry. The first section defines harmonic and often thematic opposition; the second prolongs and intensifies the tension thus created; and the third resolves this tension and ties up all loose ends. As noted, these sections are defined harmonically and thematically, but they are marked off by orchestration, rhythm, and dynamics as well. The articulation of discrete but continuous sections through thematic opposition, development, repetition, and harmonic conflict and resolution creates a self-enclosed but dynamic framework. It illustrates the hierarchical structure of patterns within patterns, as the first section, for example, is part of the A-B-A framework of the movement but has a binary form itself. The whole, when successful, attracts and holds the listener's interest through clarity and complexity of form, movement or dramatic tension, and ultimately satisfying resolution, return, and rest.

The exposition section presents one, two, or three themes and moves harmonically from the stability of the tonic key to the dissonance of the dominant (or from the minor to the relative major). In contrast to the earlier baroque style, the tension created by this initial modulation provides the driving force of the whole movement from which its large structure emerges. The arrival at the dominant key, which may introduce new themes or repeat the first with variation, is confirmed by a cadence and a change in texture that leads to the next section. The development section then fragments, recombines, deforms, or varies the themes of the first section, often playing them contrapuntally and transposing them to different keys. Agitated rhythms and sequential modulation to a variety of keys are typical of this part, creating restless movement away from the stability of the tonic or home key. The broken motifs demand thematic repetition or a return to wholeness, and the harmonic wandering requires ultimate closure so that the development ends in a climax that prepares for the final section in which this resolution will be achieved. The recapitulation repeats thematic material from the exposition in the tonic key, especially that played earlier in the dominant. The stability of this harmonic resolution is confirmed by a final cadence and sometimes by a coda, the length of this section often depending on the length of the development and its role as balance and closure to the self-contained form.

Many variations of this basic framework exist in large-scale movements and, in somewhat simpler form, in smaller movements and vocal pieces.[42] Even when the purely musical structure is of a simpler ternary, binary, or alternating (rondo) form, there may be relevant higher-order relations that add to its complexity. In a song, for example, there is the relation of music to text in addition to the relation of vocal line to accompaniment, which may be itself harmonically or contrapuntally complex. In opera, there are yet more higher-order connections and contrasts to consider: that of text to character and action (in the immediate scene and in the drama as a whole) and that between expressive qualities in the music (vocal and instrumental) and in the text. When one notes that arias may have purely musical forms of only slightly less complexity than the typical sonata form for symphonic movements, and that these must be fit into the broader tonality and expressive quality of the opera as a whole, one begins to see the complexity here in building up higher-order formal relations from more basic ones.

A major value of such recognizable forms as the sonata form described above is that they guide the perception of works that contain them, allowing audiences to grasp larger patterns and anticipate developments and resolutions to come. Listening to music with understanding is in large part a matter of having the right recollections and expectations at any given time at the proper levels of magnitude. This enables a listener to hear variations as variations, developments as developments, and returns of thematic material as such. It also facilitates or triggers those affective responses internal to the proper perception of dissonance as tension, harmonic resolution as fulfillment, and so on.

Properly hearing a musical piece is an active process that requires knowledge of forms and styles (hence of probable outcomes of what has been played and of deviations from expected continuations) and involves developing affect as well as cognition. As principles of order among elements they relate, complex formal properties enable (even as they challenge) perception and cognition to constitute these elements into larger wholes and to assign them significance in terms of their places and functions within these larger structures. The point is not to comprehend or apprehend an abstract form—one can do so more easily from a score or diagram—but to have one's listening informed by an implicit grasp of structure so as to be able to react fully to expected and unexpected developments in the music.

Part of the reward of such apprehension is intrinsic: the pleasure that contemplation of good form provides. There is probably an innate human drive to impose order on the perceived environment, to perceive closed forms and intelligible patterns. The perception of natural forms and patterns of this sort is of adaptive value in being of most service to practical reactions. Artistic forms do not serve such adaptive function. Music especially is unlike anything we encounter in the natural world, and its self-enclosed forms emphasize this separation. What constitutes a closed form in music is undoubtedly partly relative to style or convention and partly learned (even if also partly natural). Nevertheless, musical forms are, as we have seen, experienced by listeners as closed or open. And the recognition of perfect order into which all perceived elements fit, especially after being challenged by ambiguity or complexity, is naturally pleasing wherever it is found to those faculties that seek it. The pleasing effect of musical form might be heightened by its marked contrast to both nature and urban life, where the sounds we encounter are normally so seemingly random and disordered.

In general, near-perfect order is found in art, where it is placed by design, more often than in nature. Forms that exemplify it constitute one paradigm of beauty. They do not constitute the only paradigm, since natural scenes that are too complex to present perfectly intelligible order to ordinary perception and single shades of color and tones that embody no ordered relations at all may also strike us as beautiful. (For this reason, as noted much earlier, beauty is identified not by its objective side but by the reaction of pleasure its mere perception elicits.) But the pleasure derived from apprehending beautiful form is surely one type of value such forms afford.

As mentioned, an intelligible order into which all elements in a work fit also assigns those elements meaning according to their places within it. When that structure is multileveled, when it generates expressive properties and (in painting) representation that in turn enrich it at higher levels, and when perceived elements enter all these relations or levels of form, then the experience of these elements is suffused with a rich significance. In music, we hear notes and chords usually as elements within melodic and harmonic structures. Melodic phrases constantly acquire new meanings by re-presentations in altered musical contexts, some of which point ahead or thrust the listener forward and some of which resolve or fulfill what has come before. Their places in the overall structure of a movement give meaning to the occurrences of themes even as they simultaneously serve to articulate that structure.

Dewey defined aesthetic form as what generates a cumulative experience in which the perception of any part builds on the perception of others so as to constitute an ultimately all-inclusive unity.[43] This definition had its roots as far back as Aristotle, who noted that incidents in a well-constructed plot ought to surprise when they occur but at the same time appear to be logically necessitated by the characters involved and by previous episodes.[44] Both definitions of good form emphasize the interdependence of parts within it and their contribution to each other and to the overall effect or experience. Those relations that bring other parts to bear on the experience of elements within works, that kind of inner logic by which the parts seem to occur necessarily where they do, make up aesthetic form. Kant referred to this logic of aesthetic form as purposiveness without fixed purpose. It seems to be illustrated perfectly by the symphonic form described above, in which musical parts aim at resolution within the broader movement or piece as a whole, in which each element (harmonic, rhythmic, melodic) has its purpose only in its contribution to the larger form and not in any extrinsic or practical goal. The significance that each element of a piece as experienced derives from these relations is another sort of value that good form in art provides.

That the maximization of such value has been a major motive for many artists is clear once more from the history of the development of sonata form in symphonic music. Charles Rosen describes that development as in part the breakdown of horizontal and vertical lines that serve to isolate independent melodic voices and harmonic chords.[45] I can expand on this description here only in the briefest terms. The dramatic interrelation of all musical elements within the form was accomplished partly through construction from motifs that could be recognized in different contexts and combined in various ways as well as by the polarization of the large-scale harmony. In the great works of Haydn and Beethoven, the larger-scale dramatic structure mirrors melodic tensions in the individual themes and even motifs so that the former seems to grow organically from the latter.

Haydn's musical development can be seen in part in terms of the increasingly tighter relations between thematic materials in different sections of movements in his later pieces, making bridge sections less necessary. Among the numerous examples, I will mention only two: the opening movement of his *Military* Symphony, which contains two very similar themes (as is then common) and a dominant section in the exposition that begins with a repeat of the first theme, and his String Quartet op. 76, no. 2, in which the entire first movement is built from a two-note motif of a falling (later inverted) fifth.

The greater importance of the development section, in which thematic materials are fragmented and recombined or more tightly interrelated, in Beethoven's adaptations of the form is another indication of the evolution toward versions providing greater interaction among various musical elements. The nineteenth century introduced freer and looser harmonic progressions, but such composers as Dvořák and Brahms also opted for greater thematic unity across movements. As in the former's *New World* Symphony, the themes of one movement may be transformations of those in others, and themes may also be quoted or played in counterpoint across movements, tightening the overall structure at the same time as the harmonies became less predictable. Here the direction of the whole piece, and not simply of the separate movements, seems to aim at the final cadence, emphasizing once more the heightened significance that parts experienced later derive from formal relations to those experienced earlier.

I have been speaking in this section of good form, using sonata-allegro form and certain instances of it as illustration. I have also quoted from and agreed with Dewey, for whom any form that qualifies as aesthetic is good. Drawing from the brief analysis of and comments on the musical example, one might assume that a formula, or at least a set of principles, might be derived for recognizing or even producing aesthetically good form. In closing this section and anticipating some later discussion, I want to caution against such a conclusion.

It was suggested that to attract and hold our attention and interest, an aesthetic form ought to challenge our perceptual, cognitive, and affective capacities and then satisfy them in providing the sort of closed or resolved structures they seek. The sonata form, when successful, accomplishes this through a proper blend of dramatic conflict and resolution, surprise and repetition, building cumulatively toward a satisfying conclusion or closure. Attention is challenged by unexpected and novel developments within a familiar framework that includes enough repetition to prevent apparent disorder and consequent loss of interest. The dramatic form resembles that in many myths and narratives (and even in Hegelian dialectic), in which conflict and movement away from the stability of an initial equilibrium is resolved in a return to a yet more stable state that builds upon the earlier journey. The more entrenched slogan of unity in variety or complexity is applicable here, along with a mixture of familiarity with novelty and resolution or rest with tension or conflict. Unity within this form is increased by repetition, similarity, and connecting sections; variety is increased by contrast and variation.

Although the form invites these often successful mixtures, it is, of course, no formula in itself for great art. Only the relatively rare instances truly satisfy. If we speak of the proper blend of novelty and familiarity, or of unity and complexity, then we are using evaluative terms, and it takes an alchemist's trick to translate these into nonevaluative terms. The same holds true if we specify unity in terms of parts cohering or fitting better than alternatives would or in terms of subsequent parts seeming to be necessitated by what comes before. Fit is achieved sometimes by contrast, sometimes by repetition or variation, and we can formulate what is necessitated (and at the same time surprising) only partially and in the most general terms. The dominant requires a return to the tonic, but only some routes will please a knowledgeable listener. The development seemingly necessitated by an initial statement of a theme will be interesting only if the thematic material is itself of potential interest.

Unity in the nonevaluative sense can conflict with originality and expressiveness and not simply with complexity, and it takes a master to know when to unify and when to vary or contrast. Diversity is often required to hold interest, but not always. A complex and rich web of relations may generally engage us, but far simpler means may create a more striking or even seemingly mystical experience. The paintings of Mark Rothko that reduce complexity or variety almost to a minimum seem nevertheless to draw us into their vast inner spaces of pure color and hold our full attention riveted there. Yet seemingly similar monochrome paintings (those of his to which I refer are not completely monochromatic) lack the same effect.

The richest (most complex) forms do not always provide the richest experience. But those forms that do provide such experience integrate our cognitive, affective, and imaginative resources, contributing to other sources of aesthetic value and often utilizing them to build higher-order formal relations. Appreciation of form is enriched by awareness of this interaction with other sources of aesthetic value. We have noted how we experience form in music affectively and conatively in terms of building tension, delay in achievement of goals, resolution and release, and involving imagination in its anticipations or surrounding aura of musical possibilities. We have also seen how representation in painting introduces possibilities of higher-order formal relations. Form in art of any medium, as Dewey noted, is most often dynamic: It is a guide to our active perceptual processes as these integrate various faculties in grasping the many dimensions of great artworks.

[Handwritten annotations:]

physical + non-physical elements

base non-evaluative properties ← sources of aesthetic value

form, representation, expression, sensuous, historic

b.p. certain

base properties cause identity to recognize

aesthetic properties

en'up

effect

on perceptual intrpr

cognitive

affective

faculties

(all in service of form, imag)

base properties objective ↓ are by/in themselves non evaluative

↓ cause
aesthetic
properties
objective
evaluative

interpretation
enhance understanding/experience/appreciation
of artworks
by providing explanations

interpretive links description to evaluation ——
base properties with aesthetic evaluations/properties

descriptions can be true/false +
constrain interpretation

interpretation — inference to best explanation
maximize aesthetic value of work
historical relatedness of works

CHAPTER FOUR

Interpretation and History

The previous two chapters provided an account of how and why in general certain base properties that can be described without evaluation give rise to evaluative aesthetic properties—how and why the former properties are sources of aesthetic value. When it comes to particular works, the task of showing how this comes about is that of interpretation. The task of the critic is to be an interpreter, not simply to evaluate on the one hand or to describe or pick out random properties of works on the other, but to select those properties that are value relevant and to guide the audience to appreciation and proper evaluation by showing how those properties are relevant.

On the surface, those critical activities that count as interpretations of literary or other artworks make up a very diverse class. Interpreting literature may consist of giving the meanings of phrases in context, explaining the place of an episode in a plot, analyzing psychological features of characters or their motives as inferred from their actions or stated thoughts, showing formal patterns implicit in plot or character developments, stating the broad theme or historical, moral, political, or religious significance of a work as a whole, or the broader explanatory scheme (Freudian, Marxist, Christian) into which it fits. Interpretations of other artworks vary even more. An art critic or interpreter of a painting might point out how the shadows reveal diverse sources of light, what a certain interplay of colors expresses, how certain represented objects in the painting function symbolically, why certain spatial perspectives are distorted, the historical significance of the absence of traditional elements, or how the depicted relations among characters illustrate the climax of a Biblical story. A music critic will explain the place of various passages in the overall structure of a work, will describe its expressive qualities, or describe the historical importance of the work or some of its techniques in a style or tradition. Performers who are said to be interpreting musical works may simply play certain passages with emphasis or alter their dynamics or tempi slightly.

At the least, then, interpretations may state what parts or whole works mean, represent, or express, how parts relate to each other, or how works relate to others in a historical narrative. In light of the diversity of these interpretative activities, it might seem that we should heed Wittgenstein's warning and resist seeking a common core or essence. But there is a common function if not common phenomenology to these activities called interpretive outside art as well. They all seek to facilitate understanding. Interpreters who do not merely translate from foreign tongues facilitate understanding by providing explanations of various kinds. Thus if we specify the kinds of understanding and explanation at which interpretations of the arts aim, and if the kinds of understanding sought and hence explanations provided are similar across arts, then we might derive a unified account of interpretation. Again, the characteristic they share is functional: I suggested earlier in the case of music that understanding consists of the ability to appreciate. I believe that interpretation aims ultimately to facilitate appreciation in all the arts and that this is the key to its proper characterization. Furthermore, grasping what is common to interpretation across the several arts will correct some misconceptions and resolve some disputes regarding literary criticism specifically.

The Explanatory Theory

Folklore in aesthetics has it that interpretation of nonliterary art falls between description and evaluation. Evaluation depends on interpretation, which in turn depends on noninterpretive descriptions of works and their elements. The previous sentence is true; I agree that interpretation links evaluatively neutral properties that can be described without being interpreted to aesthetically evaluative properties such as grace, beauty, and power. But this does not imply a wholesale distinction between interpretation and description and certainly not one that is drawn, as is common, in epistemic terms.

Based on the fact that there is often more room for disagreement in interpretation than in noninterpretive descriptions of artworks, many philosophers claim that interpretation is invariably weaker epistemically than description, that an interpreter cannot know, or cannot knowingly know, that her interpretation is correct.[1] Descriptions, by contrast, can be known to be true.

But many of the activities described above as interpretive can produce descriptions that can be known to be true. A reader of *Death of a Salesman* and *The Prime of Miss Jean Brodie* can know that Willy Loman is self-deceptive and that Jean Brodie is manipulative, and the reader can correctly describe them as such. These descriptions are interpretations, albeit obvious ones, of the dialogue in the plays or of noninterpretive descriptions of these characters and their actions. If uniquely correct, interpretations such as these are a subclass of true descriptions, not a contrasting class (but not all interpretations, I will argue below, are uniquely correct).

How, then, do we distinguish interpretations from other sorts of descriptions and from noninterpretative encounters with artworks? Part of the distinction lies in the difference between directly perceiving and inferring. Many elements of works that we can directly perceive can be described without being interpreted. Interpretations are most often inferred on the basis of such direct perceptual encounters. In addition, elements of works that can be described without being or needing to be interpreted are those about which all observers (without perceptual defects in regard to the type of work in question) can agree (despite possibly disagreeing in interpretations of the works). Noninterpretive descriptions of artworks and their parts elicit virtually universal agreement. Hence even the direct perception of elements and their properties, if their description is a matter of dispute, counts as interpretation. Ascriptions of certain expressive properties, say, sadness in musical phrases, can fall into either class depending on context.

A central claim here is that all artistic media present us with elements that can be described without being interpreted and that such elements constrain acceptable interpretations of the works that contain them. This is perhaps most obvious in painting and music, where such directly perceivable parts include colored shapes or notes and their formal relations. As is well known, Arthur Danto has argued that visual artworks must be vehicles of interpretation in order to be artworks, since, in this age of the avant-garde, there may be physically indistinguishable objects that are not art.[2] Insofar as interpretation is required for and often implicit in appreciation of artistic values, I agree with this claim. But I want to note here that it is compatible with the fact that colored shapes are parts of paintings and can be described without being interpreted. Such elements make up the data or evidence for acceptable interpretations, which cannot be incompatible with their agreed descriptions.

If, as I claim, a unified account of artistic interpretation is possible, then there must be counterparts in literature. Given the criterion of direct perception that elicits near-universal agreement in its description, noninterpretive elements in literary art are not simply physical ink marks on paper. We do not perceive such marks and infer that they are there to represent words with meanings. Instead, we directly perceive words and sentences, and, if not defective in our understanding of the language used (e.g., English or French), we will agree on the standard meanings of these words. Having standard semantic content is part of what makes a mark or sound a word. Sometimes words are ambigious, and when they remain so in context, then interpretation is required to specify the meanings that best make sense in the work. We must infer those meanings that best explain the use of those words in those contexts. But if this were not the exception, then reading or listening would be an impossibly long and arduous task.

Ordinarily we directly perceive words as words, and we agree as to their literal meanings, which ordinarily persist in a relatively stable manner over time. This last qualifier is relevant, since the context in which words are used in literary texts includes historical context. Texts are therefore to be defined in terms of standard lexical meanings at their times of production. Those proficient in the language used in various texts are those who are familiar with the language as used at those times. When we understand the relevant language, we can agree on what the text is (in a given published edition), despite disagreeing on its proper interpretation. We can also often agree, for example, on the events described in a novel and on the ways they are literally described, despite disagreeing on the significance of those events. Texts containing such descriptions constrain acceptable interpretation in much the way that colored shapes and notes constrain interpretations of paintings and musical works.

This distinction between noninterpretive descriptions and interpretations has been challenged. Richard Shusterman, for example, argues that what we take to be descriptive fictional facts in a work depends on our interpretation of it. His example (borrowed from Richard Wollheim) is that of Hamlet's declared love for his father, which, under a Freudian interpretation, becomes a rationalization rather than a fact.[3] But what is a fact in the text is Hamlet's declaration of love for his father and the words he uses to make that declaration, however it is interpreted. There remains here, as in other conceivable examples, a level of description, a use of words with agreed ordinary meanings, that is noncontroversial.

Shusterman also points out that what descriptions we choose to pick out for attention in a work depends on our interpretation of it. This I cheerfully accept. In like manner, scientific theory guides observation and experiment, which nevertheless can be distinguished from theory and, crucially, can serve as a constraint on acceptable theories. In like manner too, those painted shapes to which we attend on a canvas will be those we take to be revelant to the significance and aesthetic value of the painting. The shapes can nevertheless be described without being interpreted. Philosophers sometimes deny distinctions simply by pointing out that one of the terms exerts an influence on the other (as in value-fact, theory-observation). But such arguments are not sound. That interpretation influences noninterpretive description does not erase the distinction between them. Interpretation can be distinguished on the other side from evaluation as well, although our interpretations will depend on which aesthetic values we take to be realizable in the perception and appreciation of the works in question.

The line between noninterpretive description and interpretation must sometimes be drawn finely, even though the distinction is real and crucial for understanding the constraints on acceptable interpretations. Some examples may help to indicate where the line lies. To point out that a musical passage leads back to the tonic key is to describe it noninterpretively, even though one requires minimal musical training to understand that description. But to claim that the passage is there simply to form a bridge back to the tonic is to interpret it, however obviously. Similarly, it was noted above that we can directly perceive without needing to interpret expressive qualities in music, say, the sadness in particular phrase. But we may need to interpret the phrase as an expression of sadness if it can be viewed and played otherwise and therefore serve a different function in the piece. Finally, to say that a character in a novel acted as he did for a particular reason may be a noninterpretive description if the action and its motive are described in ordinary terms in the novel. But it is an interpretation if it is inferred as most coherent with the explicit descriptions given the style and context of the work. Thus the same sentence may describe or interpret, depending on whether it is inferred as an explanation for what is explicitly stated in the text as opposed to its being a mere restatement.

Perhaps it should be pointed out again here that the logical relations between descriptions (which are noninterpretive), interpretations, and evaluations do not imply any order in actually perceiving and describing works of art. As noted earlier, we might first note explicitly the evaluative aesthetic properties of a work, which might suggest or even presuppose an implicit interpretation, and only later focus on those base properties that prompt our evaluative and interpretive responses. We may nevertheless use a critic's interpretation to direct or redirect our perception and appreciation of our work. The critic may well offer interpretations on different levels. She might, for example, interpret the melody beginning on C as a graceful bridge between crescendos and then interpret that graceful bridge passage as a device for producing calm hope or easing tension before the next storm.

Having located interpretation on the map with description and evaluation, we can now make explicit the account of it that has been implicit in our examples and previous discussion. It follows from that discussion that interpretation is a certain kind of inference to the best explanation. In interpreting elements of artworks we explain why they are placed in those contexts, for example, to convey a certain meaning, express a certain feeling, or lead into the development section. In interpreting whole works we explain their artistic points, why they exist as artworks, how they fit into various traditions, what artistic values they serve. The explanatory account of interpretation requires that there be uninterpreted data to be explained. In interpreting literature we seek to explain why words occur where they do, why passages constructed from them are placed where they are, why characters and events are described as they are, and so on. All this presupposes standard semantic content as part of the data to be explained. Words are to be interpreted as ironic or symbolic when we can show that the work or passage is more interesting, coherent, or expressive if those words (with those standard meanings) are understood in those ways.

The claim that interpretation is inference to the best explanation for artworks and their parts leaves open the kind of explanation at which it aims. If we held that interpreters aim at causal explanations, then we might arrive at the view that they aim to uncover artists' intentions, since these will figure prominently as causes in the production of artworks. If we held that the explanation for the use of words in a text always lies in giving their meanings, that they are placed there only to convey those meanings, then interpreting works of literature would become paraphrasing or revealing semantic content. Both these theses have been popular in accounts of literary interpretation, but it is clear, especially from the nonliterary arts, that they are at best too narrow.

In regard to the much-discussed question of intentions, there is certainly something to be said for interpreting a work as its creator intended it to be taken, if those intentions are discoverable in the work or outside it. One of the values to be derived from appreciating art is the ability to see the world of the work, and derivatively perhaps the real word as well, from another viewpoint through the imaginative eyes or genius of an artist. In all works with representional content, there is at least one implicit point of view from which that content is represented. A point of view may itself be part of the representation, and, as such, it may not always be that of the artist or author. But for a complete view of the world of a work, it is always worth asking what the artist's own view of that world is, and this normally involves thinking about the artist's intentions. If an interpreter ignores the way an artist intends her work to be understood, then he sacrifices that opportunity to see through the artist's eyes. Thus, the interpretation that captures an artist's or author's intention is not just one possible reading among others with initially equal claim. Instead it is one that has a value not realizable in other interpretations, a value that must be overridden if other interpretations are to be acceptable.

Nevertheless, that this value sometimes can and should be sacrificed to an interpretation unintended by the artist is equally clear. Considering the case of musical performance, few if any would suggest that a performative interpretation should be limited to the bounds of a composer's explicit intentions. First and notoriously, composers who conduct are not always the best conductors or interpreters of their own works. In my opinion, one may hear this firsthand by listening to Bernstein and Copeland conduct Copeland. Second, composers have intentions on different levels. Bach, for example, may have intended that a certain passage be played on particular instruments and that it produce a dramatic effect that may have been realizable on those instruments for his audience. But that dramatic effect might now require an orchestra larger than any available in his time. A contemporary conductor would then have to choose which intention to honor. Only by ignoring the broader or higher-level intention would one conclude automatically that original instruments contribute to a more "authentic" performance for a contemporary audience. Third, it is clear from the incompleteness of the notations that composers use that they do not in general intend to limit interpreters of their works by very specific intentions as to performance. Tempi, for example, could be indicated far more precisely than they usually are.

It will be objected here that musical performances are not literally interpretations in the sense specified above. Performers do not simultaneously explain what they are playing but are said to interpret simply by playing a piece with certain accents and emphases. They might be said to be interpreters only because they facilitate understanding in the way that translators of foreign languages do, by making accessible to audiences content that would otherwise be inaccessible.[4] In that case examples from performance interpretations would be irrelevant to proper accounts of critical interpretation as explanation, and this most obvious case of freedom from restriction by artists' intentions would not count in the general argument.

In defense of these examples and their implications regarding intentions as constraints, we might first try responding strongly that a performance that is genuinely interpretive might reveal an understanding of its piece that could be made explicit in an explanation of the values realized by playing it that way. We might claim on that ground that interpretations as explanations are implicit in interpretations as performances. But that claim might be too strong. First, it is doubtful that performers who are said to be interpreters must be capable of providing explanations for their ways of playing; those ways may just seem intuitively right to them. Second, even reflective critics may not be able simply to read explanatory interpretations from particular performances; the latter could be compatible with several different versions of the former.[5]

A safer answer to this objection uses the fact that interpretive performance requires understanding in a different way. Even if we cannot match such performances with verbal interpretations one-to-one, it is still the case that performances will be compatible only with certain verbal interpretations and incompatible with others. A performance is incompatible with a particular explanation of the values to be brought out in a piece if a competent musician who accepts that interpretation would not play the piece in that way. We then need maintain only that there can be acceptable performances of the same piece that are compatible only with incompatible explicit interpretations, and that composers cannot consistently intend incompatible interpretations, in order to conclude that musical interpretations are not constrained by composers' intentions. The premises are indeed plausible here. One interpretation of a piece might seek to maximize its expressive qualities by explaining various passages as means to such expression. Another might seek to make the formal structure of the piece as clear as possible. A conductor of a piece may not be able to do both at once, as can be heard, for example, by listening to performances of Brahms's Fourth Symphony by Bernstein and Szell. Once more Brahms may or may not have intended either sort of performance (he may even have written certain passages as he did simply because they seemed right to him).

Many of the points made above apply to literary interpretation and interpretation of paintings as well, although performance is of course not in question for paintings or novels. I held in the previous chapter that painters' intentions can determine which of several visually similar objects they represent. Reference to intention at that level in painting is necessary because there is no conventional system for determining reference, as there is in language and hence literature. But interpretation of visual art that goes beyond the determination of basic references for the representations requires more leeway for the viewer if aesthetic value is to be maximized. At the level of giving "deep" interpretations of a whole work (for example, in Freudian or Marxist terms or in terms of its place in a historical sequence defining a developing style), few would maintain that interpreters are constrained by artists' specific intentions along those lines. That Shakespeare could not have been capable of interpreting Hamlet himself in Freudian terms does not make that interpretation uninteresting or unacceptable. That El Greco could not have seen himself as an early expressionist does not rule out our interpreting his paintings in that way. Whether we are interpreting whole works or their parts is not really important here. Interpretation of a whole literary work, for example, requires interpretation of particular passages that is coherent with the broader account. At the more specific level, to limit interpretation to that intended by the author is to limit the values of the work for readers—to locate the source of that value entirely in the communicative act of the author when additional value can be supplied in the experience of the work by the reader as structured by a novel interpretation. Again it is not at all obvious that authors and other artists intend their works to be so limited by their narrower intentions. If artists accept (as they must) that their works may fall short of their intentions in producing them, why should they not also accept that their works may come to exceed in value their particular intentions and purposes in constructing their parts? It is plausible that most artists would intend their works to be maximally appreciated, if necessary with the aid of creative critics.[6]

Thus, the sort of explanation that we seek in interpretation is not simply causal explanation. It is rather a kind of teleological explanation. We interpret an element of a work by explaining its role in creating artistic value through its contribution to representation or content, expression, or the formal coherence of the work. We interpret a work as a whole by explaining those representational, formal, and expressive qualities that make it artistically valuable or by explaining its place in the history of the genre or in the broader culture. The purposes to which we appeal in offering such explanations (to create this or that value in the work) need not be external purposes in the mind of the artist who creates it but may be Kant's "purposiveness without purpose" internal to the structure of the work. We arrive at this conclusion by considering the fundamental purpose of interpretation itself: to guide perception toward maximal appreciation and therefore fair evaluation of a work. This purpose also generates the criterion of acceptability for interpretations. The best interpretative explanations are those that guide the perceptions of an audience toward maximal appreciation of a work, those that maximize its value for the audience.[7]

It is clear on this account that the second alternative view mentioned above (that interpretation always consists in giving meanings) must be rejected as well. Interpretation does not always consist in disclosing meanings (unless we take 'meaning' in the very broad sense of significance and equate revealing the significance of a work or its parts with explaining the value of the work or the place of its parts within its broader structure). Trivially, in the case of music and visual art, there is not always semantic content to reveal. Most interpreters of literary interpretation, however, despite disagreeing over such basic issues as whether there is one correct interpretation for each text, whether author intention is relevant, and whether interpretations are to be held true or false, agree that interpretation consists in the disclosure of meanings for texts.[8] They disagree often about the *ground* of meaning in a text, whether it is author intention, public rules of language, conventions of an interpretive community, or creative acts by readers, but in so doing they share the assumption that meaning is what interpreters are after. The ground of meaning is what philosophers of interpretation, like old-fashioned philosophers of language, seek.

This assumption must be rejected. First, if interpretation were simply the disclosure of verbal meaning, then artistic or literary value would be irrelevant, since the most probable meaning of a term or phrase in context need not be the one that maximizes its artistic value. But critics do ponder which reading makes a poem or novel most interesting or aesthetically best, especially when considering whether to interpret terms or phrases ironically or metaphorically. Second, if interpretation simply revealed meaning, then every paraphrase of a section of a literary text, no matter how short and obvious, would count as a literary interpretation. But giving the univocal ordinary dictionary meanings of the words in a simple sentence in a novel does not constitute a literary interpretation of that sentence. We need not interpret such sentences; we simply read them or grasp their meanings right off, much as we perceive trees in an eighteenth-century landscape painting without having to interpret the colored shapes as trees. Such disclosure of meaning is description, not interpretation.

I have granted that stating meaning, say, of some obscure lines in a poem, can constitute at least partial interpretation of those lines. It does so when there is an implicit claim that they contain the terms and phrases that they do in order to convey that meaning, that their value in the poem lies in conveying that meaning. Obvious dictionary meanings do not in themselves enhance literary values, and so interpretations of texts do not simply state such paraphrases. But an explanation that reveals more subtle, and perhaps controversial, meanings may add interest and value to the experience of a literary work; hence it might be an acceptable interpretation. Stating meanings will rarely constitute a complete interpretation of a text or its significant parts, since in literary art the way meanings are conveyed or presented is almost always relevant to the value of the work and hence part of the explanation for the way it is constructed. But certainly words and passages often have value in a text largely because of the meanings they convey.

Perhaps to avoid the sort of objections just raised to ordinary paraphrases as interpretations, Monroe Beardsley construes interpretation as reconstructing the meaning of a whole text or large segment from the ordinary meanings of its parts, its words and sentences.[9] But this account ignores the fact that phrases and words can be interpreted as well. It also implies that a simple paraphrase of a whole work is the paradigm interpretation of it, but it is most likely not an interpretation at all. Finally, it fails to indicate any connection between interpretation of literary arts and interpretation of nonliterary arts (those that lack semantic content). The connection is that artistic interpretation as an aid to understanding and appreciation is always explanation of the aesthetic values served by the data in the artwork that are being interpreted.

We noted above that whereas some interpretations are obvious and can be known to be true, more interesting ones are contestable. Not only are such critical disagreements more tolerable than in the case of noninterpretive descriptions, but they may also be interminable. The account offered here explains this fact as the ultimate result of differences in taste. If interpretation explains elements in works as contributing to this or that aesthetic value, if it seeks understanding in order to guide perception and facilitate appreciation of various aesthetic values, if artworks can be appreciated in different ways, if they have potential values that cannot be realized simultaneously, then there will be incompatible interpretations or explanations that appeal to different tastes or preferences for different aesthetic values. Previous examples and but little reflection suggest that the last antecedent is correct—the multidimensionality of artworks, especially very good works, makes it rare that all their potential values can be appreciated under single interpretations. This is clear in the case of performative interpretations, where a piece cannot be played in different ways at once. But it is also true of literary interpretations.

To cite some notorious cases, Henry James's *The Turn of the Screw* can be read as a ghost story or as a psychological study of a deranged woman, or it can be read as ambiguous between the two. Blake's poem *Tyger* can be read with an understanding of the tiger

as evil, as noble, or as ambiguous between the two. But in both
cases the third interpretation does not simply combine the dis-
joined previous two readings. It cannot do so if an interpretation is
intended as a guide to perception or reading. The experience of an
evil tiger as the object of the poem's vivid imagery is very different
from that of a noble one, and the experience of the poem as ambiguous is once more simply distinct from the impossible union of
the other two experiences. Similarly, the expressive atmosphere of a
ghost story is very different from that of a realistic psychological
thriller, and these qualities cannot be conjoined in a single reading
of James's novella.

Interpretations are incompatible when they ascribe, either explicitly or implicitly, properties to a work that it cannot have simultaneously. Different interpretations need not be incompatible, but they
will be when, for example, one interprets a passage as light and delicate
and another interprets it as forceful. Incompatible interpretations may
be equally acceptable when they enhance different potential values
within a work. An interpretation is acceptable when it guides an audience to an experience of a work above some threshold of value derivable from the work and when it enhances some value in the work to a
greater degree than that affordable under other interpretations.

Normally, to meet this criterion, the various parts of an overall
interpretation must cohere with each other, and they must coherently explain the values of many different parts of the work. But an
interesting interpretation might be acceptable even though it dis-
misses some parts of a work as mistakes on the artist's part, and different acceptable accounts might dismiss different elements of a
work in that way. An interpretation of *Moby Dick* as high drama
might dismiss the chapters on whales as loss of literary will on
Melville's part; an interpretation that views the story as a paean to
the power of nature might dismiss certain supernatural elements in
it instead. It always counts in favor of one interpretation over a second, however, that the former has less need to do this. Clearly according to this theory, not all interpretations or explanations of the
describable elements in a work will be acceptable, although two or
more may be. Iago's famous Credo aria in Verdi's *Otello*, for example, which is a hymn to evil, can be sung as boisterously defiant or
as broodingly sinister, but an interpretation of it as jovially comic
would be clearly unacceptable.

When we have two or more acceptable but incompatible interpretations, we cannot speak simply of truth (although we might

speak of being true to the work). Plausibility will not do either, since propositions are plausible when they are probably true under some subjective concept of probability. If incompatible interpretations cannot both be true, and if they can nevertheless be equally acceptable (with no hope of eventually finding either objectively preferable or true), then they cannot be plausible. I propose that we then speak on the first level simply of acceptability. A uniquely acceptable interpretation can be said to be true. We can also speak relativistically of truth within an acceptable interpretive scheme, and we will need to do so to construct and evaluate arguments from within such schemes. Interpretive propositions that are true within no acceptable interpretive schemes are simply false or false of the work. Once more this relativism in regard to interpretation is compatible with, and indeed ultimately reduces to, the relativity of evaluation to developed tastes that is also endorsed here.

That much art is meant to be open to a variety of interpretations is evidenced by its abundant use of metaphor and ambiguity, the incompleteness of its descriptions and/or notations, and the multiplicity but incompatibility of the values that multidimensional works can afford. The toleration of incompatible interpretations differentiates this sort of explanation both from causal explanation in the sciences and from interpretation of philosophical and other nonliterary texts. In the sciences different causes may cooperate to produce an effect, and different factors may be singled out as "the cause" of an event in different explanatory contexts, but they all must fit in principle into a single complete explanation of the effect or event. A philosophical text may be open to more than one interpretation, but ambiguity is more of a defect than a source of multiple values in nonliterary texts. To claim that art ought to communicate truth univocally is to assimilate it to philosophy (albeit of an imperfect form), an error of which both Plato and Hegel were guilty. If art communicates truth, it does so more indirectly, as I shall argue further below. And we have noted already that it challenges our cognitive faculties in other ways.

Before considering alternative views of interpretation, I should consider a broad objection that is certain to arise to the view defended here. There may appear to be clear counterexamples to the claim that interpretations of artworks aim to enhance their value or facilitate their appreciation. We might interpret a German work from the 1940s as Nazi propaganda; a feminist might interpret a work or elements within it as expressions of contempt for women;

or a historian might interpret a work as indicative of a degenerative stage of a style or tradition. In each of these cases, the interpretation, though it might be acceptable as far as it goes, would seem to lower, not enhance, the value of the work for its audience.

In response, it can be pointed out first that no such interpretation in itself can approach being a complete explanatory framework for a work with any significant potential artistic value. Claims such as the above may not even qualify as interpretations of such works as works of art. To point out, for example, that *The Merchant of Venice* is an expression of anti-Semitism or that *Huckleberry Finn* is racist (a more controversial and perhaps more interesting claim) is hardly to begin to interpret such works as literary art. Second, there are several ways in which such claims might indicate value or significance in the works to which they refer or at least valuable ways to view those works. Part of the significance of a work may lie in its being a symptom of or symbol for social attitudes prevalent at a certain time and place, however objectionable those attitudes might be. That certain elements in a work express such attitudes may, in explaining their presence there, also render explicable or comprehensive what is otherwise inexplicable, increasing the coherence if not the overall appeal of the work to its audience. Interpreting a work as an instance of a degenerating style at least indicates the sorts of aesthetic values one might seek in the work (while indicating also that an overall negative evaluation is the most one could hope for).

Interpretation, we said, links description to evaluation, and, while trying to facilitate appreciation, must sometimes dismiss or explain features of works as defects in order to generate honest evaluations. Interpretations must reveal works in their best light, but they must also be true to their character and content. They are built on accurate descriptions. Thus, the claim that interpretations of works ought to give them their best run for the money is compatible with the admission that final evaluations of them can be strongly negative and can show that others overrate them.

Other Theories

The account of interpretation as inference to value-enhancing explanations captures both the fact of incompatible but equally acceptable explanations (given different ways to enhance value) and the fact that not all interpretations are equally acceptable or acceptable at all. Whereas twenty years ago the dominant view of literary interpretation, developed by analytic philosophers, was that there is one correct interpretation for each segment of text, the current vogue is that interpretation is not constrained by independent text at all: The only constraints are those self-imposed by readers or interpretive communities. Whereas the former group tends to view interpretation as noninterpretive description, the latter assimilates it to evaluation according to particular group norms. This section will comment briefly on certain of these alternative views and their implicit criticisms of the sort of account defended above.

The denial of objective constraints from the side of the text is often part of a broader philosophical rejection of realism and foundationalism, which is skeptical of our access to any reality beyond our social verification procedures. These broader issues of truth and knowledge are beyond our context here,[10] but I shall use as our model of this view the theory of literary interpretation of Stanley Fish.[11] He denies the data base on which the explanatory account of interpretation relies. For him it is interpretive activity that creates texts with meanings. Without the contexts that interpreters supply, literary works remain indeterminate; our accepted ways of reading determine how they are to be understood. This allows, as any teacher of literature must, for better and worse readings. But acceptability here is settled by interpretive communities, by what they allow and disallow by way of interpretive strategies. To believe that texts constrain interpretations independently of such strategies is to underestimate the power of interpretive communities to license fundamentally different readings of any given work, a power evidenced both by the history of criticism and by the imaginative ingenuity of critics such as Fish.

I argued above that consideration of nonliterary arts reveals obviously the presence there of uninterpreted elements functioning as constraints on interpretation. However much interpreters may vary tempo or tone or emphasize different musical relations, they cannot ignore (at least the large majority of) the notes that confront them or alter their basic formal relations. A similar point was readily available in the case of literature. However many interpretations of Blake's *Tyger* may be forthcoming, all must confront and explain the fact that he centrally used a term that ordinarily refers to tigers. Surely this fact in itself renders certain interpretations more acceptable than others.

A defender of Fish might draw a different moral from a consideration of contemporary nonliterary art. Some contemporary painting, for example, presents minimal formal content, hence minimal constraint, to viewers or interpreters. Critics must supply significance through their interpretations, which often attribute reference to painting itself, or to its recent history and philosophy, but with a seemingly wide choice of contexts and accounts of that history. The Center for Fine Arts in Miami recently exhibited an untitled painting (1987) by Christopher Wool. It consisted of a glossy black surface of enamel on aluminum in which the viewer could dimly see his reflection. The exhibit notes read:

> In the shiny hard finish, the viewer sees himself, the lone source for any explanation of the meaning of the hermetic black color.

Although this interpretation might seem to view the painting as itself a representation of a Fishy theory of interpretation and might seem therefore, given its content, to be self-verifying, it is instead the case even here that the reflective surface must be explained and that an acceptable interpretation must indicate as much value as the painting with that surface has. Thus, if the notes had seen the viewer as the sole source of meaning for the painting rather than, as they carefully stated, of the explanation of the meaning of the painting, then the interpretation would have been self-refuting (given again its reference to the surface).

The constraints of the literary medium—basically ordinary language—are if anything stronger. But in all the arts, artists, if not critics, will attest to the resistance of the medium that constrains their avenues of communication. Indeed, a main oversight in Fish's theory is its neglect not only of the artwork itself but also of the artist, who disappears from this picture of artistic creation. The significance and value of literary works, in addition to their meaning, seem in Fish's view to be creations of critics and their interpretive communities. It must be so if their interpretations remain unconstrained by authors' texts. Fish writes:

> No longer is the critic the humble servant of texts whose glories exist independently of anything he might do; it is what he does, within the constraints embedded in the literary institution, that brings texts into being. . . . The practice of literary criticism is not something one

must apologize for; it is absolutely essential not only to the mainte-
nance of, but to the production of, the objects of its attention.[12]

The neutral reading public may think this thesis places the bulk of
the credit for great literary works in the wrong quarter.

Fish often relies for his theory's defense on the theoretical claim
that meaning is created through institutional practice rather than
residing transcendentally in language or texts independent of practice.[13] This claim is not disputed. The response is that those fundamental practices that create cores of stable meanings for terms are
not the practices of literary criticism or even writing literature. The
writer as well as the critic uses a language that is ready-made
through earlier social practice. The writer can stretch or add to the
language, but only parasitically on earlier use. The critic confronts
language in particular texts that use it in specific ways, and she must
explain those uses. The distinction between creative artist and critic
is real and sharper than Fish in his passionate defense of the critic
allows.

The final complaint against his theory has to do with standards.
As noted, for him interpretive communities set the standards for
acceptable critical interpretations.[14] This metanormative thesis allows that some groups of interpreters are better at their practice
than others only according to their own standards, leaving all
groups with equal status, that is, without objective criteria for critical standards themselves or ultimately for acceptable interpretations. In practice, of course, no literature teacher would or should
admit that a stable group of high school students with common
standards and methods of interpretation for collaborating on their
homework has the same claim to acceptable interpretation as the
best critics. However, if, like Fish, we locate interpretive authority
in the community of recognized professional critics, then we have
the problem of the gifted but unrecognized amateur. What makes
such a critic gifted is the acceptability of his interpretations, his offering novel explanations that show how to understand parts of the
work in ways that enhance their values. Meeting this criterion of
adequacy to text does not await recognition from the community of
professional critics. In elevating the status of critics to artists, Fish's
theory destroys their status as critics (except according to their own
idiosyncratic standards and academic or publishing positions).

On the other side of the line from our intermediate position is
the thesis that interpreters must reveal the intentions of artists as

the criterion of the uniquely correct interpretations of their works. I rejected above both the idea that there normally are uniquely correct interpretations of multivalued works and the claim that interpreters are constrained by artists' intentions (although I accepted that seeing the world of a work through its artist's eyes or intentions is one major value among others to be derived from it). Here I want to consider in somewhat more detail the arguments of the proponents of intentionalism and a counterexample proposed to my account.

E. D. Hirsch, the champion of the intentionalist theory of interpretation, relies mainly on the argument that only consideration of authors' intentions can make the meanings of literary texts determinate. According to his view, if there is to be a standard of correct interpretation, it must lie in the determinate meaning of the text. And if meaning is to be determinate, it must be made so by the author's intending a determinate meaning, since texts in themselves may be interpreted in radically different ways.[15]

One can dispute the degree of determinacy in ordinary discourse and expository writing, where context and conventional content normally make it quite clear what is being said by making it overwhelmingly improbable that anything else could be meant. In much poetry and some other literary forms, it might seem that we must grant Hirsch his indeterminacy thesis. Even here, however, the claim should not be that the ordinary meanings of the words or phrases used are unclear but instead that the broader themes understood to be asserted by those words, the proper explanations for their uses in those contexts, are not uniquely determined by the texts themselves. In this sense ordinary meanings do not constrain us to a single interpretation, a thesis that Hirsch correctly shares with his rival Fish against Beardsley. Author intention, when discoverable and added to verbal context, is the means, according to him, to make texts that are indeterminate in this way determinate and to avoid the chaos that Fish's sort of theory entails. Assuming for the moment that interpreters do seek to specify meanings in this broader sense, is intention the key to such specification?

One might first accuse Hirsch and other intentionalists of confusing utterance meaning with speaker's meaning. This is now a common distinction in philosophy of language, and it is implicit in the possibility of failed linguistic intentions on the part of speakers. Speakers can fail to say what they intend to say if they use words improperly, and then their meanings, what they intend to convey, will not match the meanings of their utterances, what fully competent listeners would construe them as saying. The extreme result of ignoring this distinction entirely is the Humpty Dumpty theory of meaning, according to which speakers can make their statements mean whatever they like. Hirsch is not guilty of this extreme (and extremely silly) theory, since he allows that semantic conventions constrain what can be conveyed or meant by the use of words.[16] But there is still a confusion in this vicinity in Hirsch's main argument.

The intention of a speaker cannot in itself alter her utterance meaning, and so we cannot, as Hirsch implies we should, make utterance or textual meaning determinate by taking into account author intention if that meaning is otherwise indeterminate. We can, however, substitute author (speaker's) meaning for textual (utterance) meaning if the latter is indeterminate and the former is independently discoverable. This would not in itself make the text a satisfactory work if determinacy in its meaning is required for that, but it might make the experience of the work more satisfactory, and we might now charitably interpret Hirsch as advocating this move.

I argued above, however, that constraining interpretations within the bounds of artists' intentions denies to audiences certain values that may be derivable from works although not explicity foreseen or intended by their creators. This is certainly true at the level of explaining the significance of various events as described in a work or at the broadest level of choosing an overall explanatory framework. If *The Turn of the Screw* makes an interesting work under a naturalistic (as opposed to supernaturalistic) framework, or *Hamlet* can be understood and explained in detailed Freudian terms, these interpretations would not be ruled out by the recognition that their authors did not or even could not have intended them. The same point holds in regard to the significance of particular words and phrases in such texts. In fact, the narrower point follows from the broader claim, since interpreting entire texts in different ways will entail interpreting some of their parts differently. By contrast, the ordinary meanings of the terms even in abstruse works are ordinarily determinate enough or, if ambiguous in context, remain so whatever the intentions of their authors. Thus, Hirsch's appeal to author intention as a constraint on interpretation is often either useless or pernicious if heeded.

In ordinary contexts of communication, we do not use speaker's meanings to get at utterance meanings, as Hirsch implicitly suggests

that we should in understanding literary art. In everyday communication it is the other way around: We use utterance meaning as determined by semantic conventions to grasp what a speaker is trying
to convey to us. The best argument for intentionalism in the theory
of interpretation holds that art is a kind of communication or conversation, in which we try to understand what artists are saying to
us by recovering their intentions from their works, much as we do
in ordinary contexts. Noël Carroll provides this argument in his recent defense of intentionalism. He specifically emphasizes our conversational interest in art and holds that this interest can trump
other aesthetic values that we might derive from various works.[17]

As noted several times above, I do not deny this interest, but I
do deny that it functions as a constraint on acceptable interpretations. The interest in what an artist is trying to say, when this does
not uniquely match what we can take her work to be saying, indicates one sort of value to be derived from the work. But this value is
neither absolute nor lexically prior to others according to my account. Nor are the intentions of artists to say specific things in their
works the only relevant ones. They may also intend us to appreciate their works to the fullest, which may require creative responses
on our part. Between these broad and specific intentions may be
others. Artists may try to instill in us a different view of our society,
to prompt us to reform certain institutions, and so on. But when
they try to get us to do such things, they do so indirectly, by getting
us to appreciate the worlds of their works and make the relevant
comparisons to the worlds in which we live. The broad, direct intention seems paramount from the artistic point of view.

What makes the context of art different from ordinary contexts
of communication to which Carroll assimilates it is the intention
and need to have works appreciated in addition to having artists understood. This difference is why the manner of communicating is
always as important as the content communicated in art. The appeal
to intention as a constraint does not err in forcing us outside the
work in search of its proper interpretation. We must in any case
view the work in its proper historical context to interpret and appreciate it fully. Nor is the problem that artists' intentions are inaccessible. We must ascribe intentions to others all the time in interpreting not only their language but also their behavior in general.
The problem is only that the appeal is too limited and ascribes too
much importance to certain inferred specific intentions on the part
of artists.

Carroll offers an example, however, that is aimed directly at the sort of theory defended here. It is designed to show that the conversational interest in recovering an artist's intended communicative content does indeed trump or constrain our interest in interpreting a work so as to make it as good as possible, so as to derive maximal aesthetic value from it. His example is that of a hack Hollywood film by a second-rate director that contains choppy editing and other amateurish techniques. The film would seem better, its aesthetic value increased, Carroll argues, if it were viewed as a bold, avant-grade attack on Hollywood norms of filmmaking, à la Godard at a later period. But that would be a wrong, that is, unacceptable, interpretation, since it is obvious that the director intended no such attack on the methods he in fact so unsuccessfully tried to imitate. Hence fidelity to the artist's intention does constrain our charitable instinct to view his work in the best light possible.[18] Again we seem to have a counterexample to the central claim that interpretation aims to facilitate maximal appreciation of works.

I agree that interpreting this film (as Carroll describes it) as an avant-garde attack on Hollywood norms would be incorrect or unacceptable, but not because of any general constraint to be true to artists' intentions. There is one factor that makes this example atypical and one way in which I disagree with Carroll's assessment of the alternative interpretations here. The differentiating factor is that the notion of "avant-garde attack" is itself an intentional notion, and the revelant intention is not the sort of purpose internal to a work that I described above. The question here is whether this director's editing methods were mistakes or intentional transgressions, and to answer that we can only surmise about his intentions. My account does not suggest that we falsify these in order to make a work seem better.

The deeper question here is whether the experience of this work really would be better if we thought that the disconcerting techniques were intentional affronts to the film establishment. Interpretation, I have maintained, is a guide to experiencing a work so as maximally to appreciate its value. Recognition of an interesting relation to a tradition may enliven the perception of a work whose qualities are interesting in themselves. But to think that all deviations from established methods, even when they are intentional, indicate positive values, is to place too high a value on mere originality. I shall have somewhat more to say on the value of originality in general below, but in this case I doubt that interpreting as intentional deviations features of a film that appear to be mistakes precisely because they make the experience of it so unsatisfying would make that experience any better. Hence I deny that this example shows us that we must honor artists' intentions at the expense of more satisfying experiences of their works.

One other intentionalist account should be mentioned here. According to this view, the proper interpretation of a text seeks not the actual intention of its author but the intention that an intended reader is most justified in ascribing on the basis of available evidence.[19] An author's secret or hidden intentions are here taken to be irrelevant. With sufficient charity to the author to whom these hypothetical intentions are ascribed, this theory comes closer to the one advocated here. But it still fails to draw a sufficient distinction between utterance or text meaning and speaker's meaning. If one can fail to say what one intends, or say more than one intends, then one's utterances or texts can contain unintended meanings, and there can be meanings that we are not justified in ascribing to an author.[20] Suppose, for example, that a text fails to say what its author intends, but she makes that intention clear in a published letter. Then to limit acceptable interpretations to what available evidence justifies us in ascribing to the author once again denies to readers experiences of the work guided by explanations of how its parts can contribute to its overall value.

Our account neither grants to readers as interpreters the freedom to compose their own texts from associations prompted by the actual texts before them nor makes literary and other artworks the exclusive mental property of their creators. It recognizes that when artworks leave their creator's hands, they enter the public domain demanding recognition and explanation as they are. The account maintains the line between explaining the value of a work as we encounter it and creating a new or different work. It avoids the intellectual chaos that results from ignoring the demand to be true to the work in acceptable interpretations, the confusion of substituting the critic for the artist, without substituting the artist for the work. It recognizes the value of seeing as the artist saw and the challenge to our cognitive powers to appreciate that value without elevating it to absolute status in aesthetic contexts. Most important, it accommodates the diversity of interpretive activities and acceptable interpretations without abandoning standards of adequacy to text or work.

Filling Out Worlds of Representational Works

One further test for theories of interpretation is their implications for filling out worlds of representational or fictional works, for determining which propositions not explicitly stated in those works are nevertheless true in those worlds. It is fictionally true, for example, that Sherlock Holmes has an obsessive personality and also true (to borrow an example from David Lewis) that he lives closer to Paddington than to Waterloo Station, although neither proposition is stated explicitly in the texts of the stories. When we read a fictional work, we expand the text into an imaginary world by adding imaginatively to what we are explicitly told. The question is how we do this, according to what principles. The answer, I believe, is that we follow our interpretations of the work, our best explanations for the text as it is written. The first statement about Holmes made above, for example, is a straightforward interpretation of his character whereas the second, although probably not explicitly part of any acceptable interpretation (and therefore not entertained by any reader save Lewis), follows from the text and its acceptable interpretations (specifically, from the proposition that Holmes lives on Baker Street and from the interpretive claim that the London portrayed in the text is the real London of the time).

We can then test a theory of interpretation by seeing whether propositions held true in various fictional worlds according to interpretations of the text that are endorsed by the theory are plausibly held true in those worlds. My claim is that the most plausible ways to expand upon texts (and representational paintings) follow from the theory of interpretation defended here. Other principles have been proposed but are easily found wanting. Let us compare their capacity to capture examples against our theory's.

Two principles first proposed by David Lewis have been widely considered. One has us fill out what is explicitly stated in a fictional text with truths from our real world. Roughly, what is true in the world of the fiction is what is true in the closest possible world to ours in which the story is told as known fact.[21] The second principle fills out fictional worlds to be consistent not with the real world but with what their authors and intended audiences believed, so that, for example, it is fictional in a medieval work that the world is flat. The second principle allows us to view the world of a work through the eyes of its author whereas the first makes the world more familiar to us.

These principles are too rich in the worlds they generate. The worlds of fictional works are only partial (compared to the usual sense of 'possible worlds'). In incorporating truths in accordance with these principles, we consider only propositions that are explanatorily linked in some way to those in the text. In incorporating truths from the real world, for example, we do not consider it true in the world of Bertie Wooster that the invention of the cotton gin antedated that of the radio by 103 years (nor false in that world either). But it is true there, although not explicitly stated in the Wodehouse texts, that Cannes is a resort city in the south of France and that Harrod's is a department store in London. These propositions are true in that world because the best explanation for the use of these names in the text is to refer to the real city and store in question. Thus, it appears already that a deeper principle appealing to explanations of the text is at work.

Second, even if these principles were jointly sufficient, in that fictional truths not explicitly stated were derived only from the real world or from beliefs of authors and their intended audiences, it seems we would still need a deeper principle to tell us when to use one or the other. Holmes lives closer to Paddington than to Waterloo even if Conan Doyle and his audience were ignorant of the geography of the London train system. We use the truth from the real world here because, as maintained above, it is explanatorily linked to the text via its acceptable interpretations. By contrast, a Russell's viper can climb a rope in the world of Sherlock Holmes (as it cannot in the real world) not simply because Conan Doyle believed that but because it is necessary to Holmes's really having solved the case of the speckled band, to the obvious interpretation of the denouement of that story.

Third, these principles are not sufficient. What is true in the world of fantasies or supernatural tales is what is consistent with the best readings of those works as fantasies. Such worlds may be distant from the real world and from the beliefs of authors and intended readers. There may be ghosts in the world of *The Turn of the Screw*, even though there are none in the real world, and neither James nor people literate enough to read him believe in them. There are ghosts in that world (under some acceptable interpretations) if the interpretation of relevant passages as referring to or implying their presence enhances some major value of the work, say, its atmospheric or expressive power. Once more, whether we ascribe fictional truths that are not explicit in texts in accord with these principles depends on interpretive, value-enhancing explanations.

In another example, this time from Nicholas Wolterstorff, it may be that in the real world a relationship such as Mark Twain describes between Huck Finn and Jim would include homosexual activities. But it is not true in their world that their relation is homosexual.[22] We do not apply the Reality Principle, as Kendall Walton calls it. Why not? It is not because Twain or his audience did not believe in homosexuality. Instead we do not ascribe in accord with the Reality Principle because it is no part of a best explanation for the descriptions of the relation in the text that these descriptions indicate sexual preference. Such an explanation would be inconsistent with the moral tone of the work and its broader themes. It would complicate those themes, introducing a distracting foreign element that would detract from most readers' experience of the work.

Kendall Walton provides a final example in which our ascriptions of fictional truths accord with neither principle. He cites a reader concluding from subtle clues in the text of a Conrad story that a character has committed suicide when no one in real life, either in Conrad's time or at present, would draw that inference or be warranted in doing so on such slim evidence. Walton concludes from the insufficiency of these principles that we require a multiplicity of divergent principles without any overarching meta-rule for determining when to use them.[23] He offers a Wittgensteinian response to the question of how we can operate with such a divergent set to arrive at agreement on what is true in various fictional worlds. The response consists in pointing out that many concepts must be applied without governing rules.[24] But the concept of fictional truth is not like the concept of red in this respect. The former is not a concept that we see immediately to be applicable in such a way as to rule out rational debate. To settle such critical debate, we need a guiding rationale, and our theory of interpretation provides it. Walton's example provides further evidence of this. We infer the suicide of the character in Conrad's story because that is the only explanation for the clues in the text being placed there at all.

The theory also explains why many of the questions characterized by Walton as silly do not arise for literary or other representational works. We do not ask why Othello, a Moorish general, speaks such fine English poetry because the purpose of or explanation for his lines being written in that way is not to represent his style of speaking. Thus it is not fictionally true that he speaks in that way. Similarly, the explanation for artificial poses and positions of figures in Renaissance paintings most often appeals to formal beauty and expressive power, not to representational accuracy. That is why we need not ask why Leonardo's diners at his *Last Supper* are all lined up on the same side of the table.

One other more recently proposed principle for generating fictional truths should be mentioned here, that of Gregory Currie. According to Currie, when we read a work of fiction, we imagine not only that the story is true but also that someone is telling it to us—a fictional author. What is true in the story is what the fictional author believes. This figure is to be distinguished from a narrator, who is fallible, and from the real author, who does not believe what is written in the text.[25] There is once more much overlap between the application of this test for fictional truth and the ascription of such truths in accord with value-enhancing interpretations. If we posit a fictional author, then we will normally seek to make the beliefs of this figure coherent, for example, and coherence is also normally an aesthetic value in a fictional work. But there are also cases, including some of those mentioned above, where these criteria come apart or where there seems to be little if any room in our make-believe world for the fictional figure that Currie builds into his principle for generating fictional truths there.

An author, fictional or not, who is intelligent enough to write *The Turn of the Screw* would not believe in ghosts. Hence Currie's criterion would once more wrongly rule out reading the novella as a ghost story. Sherlock Holmes lives closer to Paddington than to Waterloo whether or not Conan Doyle, his audience at the time, or a fictional author of that time, were all ignorant of geography. It is fictionally true in the Holmes stories that the highly fallible Watson is telling them. Conan Doyle really tells them. Is there room for us to imagine that there is a third teller of the stories? And is it plausible that we utilize such a complex scheme in generating the fictional truths of Holmes's world? Our best readings or interpretations of the works are readily available, by contrast, since we are always interpreting as we are reading. In other fictional media, such as movies, it is often doubtful that it is fictionally true that anyone is telling us a story: We simply see the fictional events unfold before us. If we were to imagine learning of these events only secondhand, this might lessen our direct involvement in the world in which they take place—a directness that is an aesthetic virtue of this particular medium.

We may conclude that our theory of interpretation generates fictional truths in accord with our actual practice as opposed to other proposed principles. These truths are consistent with value-enhancing explanations for revelant passages in fictional works. We have used the criterion for fictional truth as a test for the theory that views interpretation as a means to the appreciation of aesthetic value. That it passes this test helps to show once more that interpretation is indeed the link between description and evaluation of artworks.

Historical Relativism

Historical considerations must enter the picture at this point for two reasons. First, I have claimed that interpretations link particular instantiations of base properties to evaluative aesthetic properties in works by showing how the former contribute to the values that help to constitute the latter. But which evaluative properties a work has, and so how the base properties determine those features for various critics, turns out to be relative to standards that can change with historical developments within and among different styles. Hence the interpretation of local objective characteristics of works as contributing to such evaluative properties as grace, power, or beauty—properties that do not seem to include or depend on historical relations—turns out surprisingly to depend on the work's place in a historical tradition or style. Various puzzles arise from such historical relativity of standards that must be addressed here.

Second and less surprising is the dependence of global interpretations of whole works on their historical contexts. I have said that one major type of such interpretation refers to the significance of works for later ones and in relation to earlier ones. There can be no doubt that some works are valuable and highly regarded because they strongly influence the development of a style, foreshadow much later developments in art, bring an existing tradition or set of aesthetic ideals to its conclusion or ultimate fruition, or alter the course of art history. Their interpretations will aim to show how and why this is so. Such historical relations, once recognized, add value to the works they connect because they enable us to understand features of the later works as logical developments from those of the earlier works. We value such understanding as a successful answer to the challenge to our cognitive powers presented by many artworks. Answering this challenge is part of the enjoyment we derive from the appreciation of art and is one of the reasons why we study art history.

Global interpretation need not always relate works to others, however. Works may also be significant because of their place in the broader culture or social setting of the time and place, and their interpretations can place them in this sort of broader context. They may have global significance in other ways as well. Representational works are about something concrete and often more abstract as well, and they are typically interpreted in those terms. Nonrepresentational works may be about something also, although what they are typically about is some aspect of the tradition into which they fit. Some of the earliest purely abstract works in painting, for example, can be interpreted to be about the history of painting, the nature of the medium, and the proper goals of this art form. Most of these types of interpretation, then, refer directly or indirectly to historical traditions in art or broader culture, and questions again arise regarding the stability of the values served by works located in their historical contexts and of the interpretations that aim to facilitate appreciation of those values.

Let us first consider the problems of local interpretation of elements within works as contributing to their historically relative evaluative properties. The ascription of such properties by knowledgeable critics changes over the course of time and in the face of later artistic developments, and this can create philosophical confusion. When evaluative properties, and the interpretation of base properties as contributing to them, seem to change because of the creation of later works, this can seem as mysterious as backward causation. Anita Silvers cites the example of Rubens figures, which were considered coarse at the time he painted them but later recognized as elegant, after acceptance of figures such as those of Picasso.[26] An example of a change in the opposite direction, probably more typical if less noted, would be musical compositions of the earliest classicists, which sounded graceful at the time but were later revealed by Mozart's perfect grace to be rather awkward and groping. To say simply that such properties of works change when other works are created later, and to leave it at that, is to invoke what looks like sheer magic.

One metaphysically more conservative alternative maintains that evaluative properties must inhere in works from the time of their creations, even when those properties come to be noticed or appreciated only later in light of further artistic developments and even if they could be known only in retrospect.[27] According to this position, the works of the Mannheim School referred to above were always awkward, although this property could not be heard until later, when the compositions of Haydn and Mozart were available for comparison. This claim implies, however, that the critics of the earlier time were simply mistaken, and that seems a harsh judgment. To say they were mistaken is to say that these contemporaries of Stamitz should have foreseen Mozart or that their mistake was inevitable. But if Mozart had never composed, would they still have been mistaken? Must critics conceive of every possible ideal composer and piece in order to offer acceptable interpretations and correct evaluations? This would be an impossible standard for real critics to meet. The result of applying it would seem to be skepticism regarding the acceptability of any actual interpretation or evaluation at any particular time. Such thoroughgoing skepticism seems no better than the apparent backward causation of the alternative position. Thus we seem to have a dilemma here.

Neither the threat of skepticism nor the threat of an absurd metaphysics is as bad as it at first appears, however; this dilemma can be seized by both horns. Even allowing that evaluative properties of works change when later works alter the relevant standards, we can dispel the illusion of backward causation by simply noticing once more that these properties are relational. Relations change when new elements of the relations come into existence even when the original elements remain the same. Earlier I analyzed evaluative aesthetic properties in terms of relations to responses of ideal critics. Such critics will apply standards in responding evaluatively to the objective or base properties of works, and so the evaluative properties they ascribe are relative to these standards as well. If the standards of even ideal critics change over time, then the evaluative properties that are relative to these standards will change as well, without requiring any mysterious causal relations between later works and earlier ones.

But if we analyze such properties as grace as relational properties presupposing some standard, such as the property of tallness or shortness in persons, an epistemological problem remains in the aesthetic context that differentiates it from others involving properties such as height. A tall person in 1300 might be short in 1995, but the standard measures still allow us to know just what height that person is. But in the case of aesthetic properties there are no obvious standards that allow us to know at any given time just how graceful or awkward a piece of music is. To claim only that each work retains whatever degree of grace or awkwardness it has when created even though we have no convenient way to specify that degree leaves open the skeptical question of what the unspecified standard could be. And without some such standard, we cannot know whether a work is awkward or graceful.

Is grace in music to be measured in relation to Mozart's compositions (even before he wrote them?) or in terms of what might ideally have been written in the style of the piece under consideration? This question can be translated into the terms of our earlier framework by asking whether ideal critics, who ascribe evaluative properties to which base properties are interpreted as contributing, are to be conceived as having knowledge of the entire future as well as history of art from their temporal viewpoint. If we grant ideal critics such knowledge and judge truth in ascription of evaluative properties in relation to their responses, then it once more seems that we cannot judge the interpretations and evaluations of real critics. This standard for evaluative properties would seem to demand that critics be ideal composers themselves, a demand so stringent as to result once more in full skepticism. Leaving the standard unspecified is, as we have seen, epistemically no better. The third and most natural alternative is to allow the standard for measuring grace and other evaluative properties to change over time as new compositions appear more or less graceful than earlier ones. Here we grant ideal critics knowledge of the history but not of the future of their art. Although this theory is perhaps more natural in bringing ideal critics closer to real ones, it seems to leave us still no better off epistemically, since we could still never be sure that future compositions would not alter ascriptions of these properties to the same works. It appears in this light that the best we can do is to relativize explicitly ascriptions of evaluative properties and interpretations that depend on them to standards operative at a time, recognizing that new relevant standards will likely emerge in the future.

The historical context for interpretation and evaluation may not be so bleak, however. First, as time passes we may become more confident that developed standards applied to works of earlier eras will not alter with future developments. This appeal to the test of time remains to be assessed. Second and related, the recognition of distinct styles that dominate for a time but then are forever super-seded by others actually provides a more rather than less stable framework for interpretation and evaluation. To see why this is so, we must briefly define the parameters that define the identities and progressions of artistic styles.

Styles

The identification of a style involves first noting the recurrence of patterns across different works that serve to differentiate them from others. These patterns may result from any use of a medium that creates formal, expressive, or representational properties. If stylistic, these properties are taken to be characteristic of an artist, school, movement, region, or era, to express a distinctive point of view associated with any of the above. Stylistic qualities are not simply any properties that serve to identify an artist's work. Such properties might include the way an artist signs her name, which, if not integrated into the form or content of a work, is not part of its style. Stylistic properties must contribute to the overall appearance of a work or group of works as artworks. They must be evalua-tively significant, involve the employment of artistic norms is some way, and contribute to the creation of aesthetic properties in the works.[28]

We may divide such norms into constraints, ideals, and strategies for realizing these ideals. Their use explains the recurrence of stylis-tic patterns that differentiate groups of works from others. They need not be employed consciously or intentionally by artists: Even if Van Gogh had not intentionally employed his brush strokes for expressive effect, they certainly would constitute part of his style because of their distinctiveness and contribution to expression in his paintings. As an illustration of the division of norms specified above, we may again use musical composition in the classical style of Haydn and Mozart. An example of a constraint here would be the sonata-allegro form for most opening movements of major symphonic works. (To call a form a constraint is not to imply a lack of innovation or variation in its employment.) Ideals would include the expression of dramatic tension and resolution as well as symme-try, grace, and clarity in form. Major strategies for realizing these ideals included the development of recombinable and variable melodic motifs that implied the dramatic harmonic opposition of the tonic and dominant.

The most important point for our purposes here is that different styles or traditions of musical composition and painting establish different goals or ideals for artists who work within them, and they suggest possible ways of realizing these goals. The ideals and the styles they help to define may be as broad as that of realistic depiction in painting, which spanned the Renaissance through Constable and Delacroix to the contemporary photorealist style, or as narrow as Constable's own problem of capturing sunlight in his landscapes. But in each case they provide their own standards of evaluation applicable to works in those styles and traditions. It therefore may be possible at least in restrospect to establish the historical culminations of particular styles, especially those defined by more specific ideals, constraints, and strategies, and hence to be confident that measures of value-relevant properties implicit in the stylistic ideals will not be supplanted. The pure classical style of musical composition could not improve upon or even extend beyond Mozart. Beethoven seemingly had to push beyond that style, and Prokofiev much later could only mimic it in his first symphony. Hence it seems perfectly safe to measure the evaluative aesthetic properties of works in that style against now well entrenched if historically relative standards.

From the point of view of our framework, it therefore makes little difference whether present ideal critics who ascribe such evaluative properties to works of that period are granted knowledge of the future as well as the past, symphonic repertoire. We can safely assume that the future will not alter the standards for composition in that style and others that continue to elicit our attention and admiration but no longer guide the creation of new works. When real critics interpret and evaluate elements within works, they bet that the standards they implicitly apply will not prove historically vulnerable, and when they also relativize to standards implicit in particular styles, they are often right. When standards do change for works within a developing style, it again makes little difference whether we say that the relational evaluative properties themselves change or that the earlier critics or criticisms were mistaken. Both ways of speaking make sense if they indicate the crucial fact of changing norms.

The problem of historical relativism becomes more pronounced, however, when we shift attention from the interpretation of particular elements within works as contributing to historically relative evaluative properties to the interpretation of whole works in terms of their historical significance. Thus far we have pointed only to relations among artworks themselves as pertinent to ascriptions of evaluative properties to the works. Our problem lay in the extent to which we may be unable to predict those future developments that might render past works more or less valuable. But it is a short step from recognition of the effects of later works in altering standards for interpreting and evaluating earlier ones to the claim that the value of whole works is a function of those narratives that art historians devise to classify earlier works with later ones. If such narratives are original and peculiar to particular art historians, and if interpretations of works depends on their incorporation into one such narrative or another, then such interpretation and evaluation become purely subjective and not simply historically relative. Indeed we do find very different styles of art history. The same paintings may be interpreted in different periods as symptoms of their artists' personalities, as formal structures, as allegories, as political statements.[29] When they receive such different interpretations, they will be linked with different groups of works in different narratives.

Art historical narratives of the same time span differ not only because historians can pick and choose different causal sequences for emphasis but more emphatically because real causal connections do not seem necessary for works or artists of different periods to be related in narratives. It was not necessary for Giotto to influence causally the work of Cézanne, for postimpressionist critics of formalist bent to see him as a prophet of formalist ideals and to elevate his reputation at so late a time. El Greco stands in a similar relation to twentieth-century expressionist painting according to some art historians' narratives, and again the question whether modern expressionists intentionally sought to extend El Greco's artistic ideals (or those of artists directly influenced by him) seems beside the point. Of course, even if historians had to establish a case for actual influence through some chain of artists' intentions as a basis for their narratives, there would remain much room for diversity, since causal relations spread almost ubiquitously and evidence for intentions is generally sketchy and indirect in any case. But just as artist intention does not constrain the interpretation of single works, so it fails to impose a constraint on art historical narratives that link various works together. And without any pretext of this constraint, it may seem yet clearer that selection of artworks for inclusion in narratives, and hence for ascription of historical significance, depends mainly on the interests and tastes of historians.

We could have predicted this variance in art historical narratives from the terms of our previous analyses. General styles, it was held, are constituted by overlapping patterns of evaluatively significant properties in works. But evaluatively significant properties are relative to the tastes of the critics or art historians who ascribe them. Art historians will therefore vary in picking out the most significant stylistic features of works from among those that could be taken to define the styles according to which they group various works. This can lead to suspicion among aestheticians of the category of general as opposed to individual style. Some hold that whereas individual style is a real causal effect of the psychology of individual artists, general styles that group works across artists are merely subjective schemes of classification imposed by art historians.[30]

The abandonment of the Hegelian idea of a single teleological progression to one inevitable conclusion to the history of art can lead to the extreme alternative idea of only multiple subjective narratives linking various works. But can we again find a more plausible middle ground in the concept of real stylistic connections among works? Here we would substitute for the concepts of a fixed goal and necessary progress toward it those of local goals of various styles. On the other side, we would substitute for the purely subjective standard of consensus among groups of art historians at a time the requirement that they make plausible cases for real stylistic, if not causal, relations among the works they connect in their narratives. As argued earlier, mere subjective consensus cannot constitute a criterion of correct interpretation. Regarding historical interpretation—the ascription of historical significance to works— only competent and knowledgeable critics could count toward establishing standards for acceptable narratives and the works they incorporate. But competent art historians are not simply those approved by other members of some group to which they belong. Instead, they are those who can recognize genuine historical developments when they find them.

In favor of the view that general styles are as real as individual styles is first the fact that the former seem to develop in ways similar to Aristotle's aforementioned description of good plot developments in tragedy. In both domains, later stages in retrospect seem implicit in or necessitated by earlier stages, even though they cannot be predicated in advance and hence seem novel and exciting when they occur. That such sequences appear logically necessary from later viewpoints indicates that they constitute real if not wholly objective constraints on art historical narratives. They are not wholly objective because the order of such sequences is specified in psychological and aesthetic rather than in physical, causal terms. As Arthur Danto points out with only slight hyperbole, beginnings, endings, and turning points are not in the world but in human stories.[31] Nevertheless, general styles and the connections they comprise seem real because, as noted above, those ideals established early in their development, which remain internal to them and partly constitutive of them, may be unquestionably fulfilled later on. The modern historian of music, and even the moderately knowledgeable listener, cannot help but hear the music of Stamitz as a precursor to that of Mozart and judge it in that light. To whomever else Stamitz may be connected in some future and presently unexpected narrative, he will always be connected to Mozart as well.

The second source of support for this view is the fact that individual artists undoubtedly accept the same ideals, constraints, and even strategies as certain of their predecessors. These defining features of general styles can certainly be operative within groups of artists. In that sense, general styles are real to artists themselves. We must note again, however, that the acceptance of constraints and ideals by artists does not constrain critics or art historians in their interpretations. Historians can discover unintended connections and can discount the significance of those that are intended by artists. Having duly noted this point here, however, we may recognize that it carries less weight than in the earlier context. The claim here need not be that historians are constrained in their interpretations by those ideals, constraints, and strategies consciously adopted by artists, but instead that when such patterns function across individual artists' works, they make available stable frameworks for assigning art historical significance to those works. Such frameworks are discovered, not invented by historians. Gifted historians are not those who invent the most original narratives. They are those who find (and make plausible cases for) genuine stylistic relations across time where others saw only isolated artistic episodes.

Given the availability of stable historical frameworks provided by stylistic connections across the works of different artists, the historical significance of a work may more firmly entrench its evaluative status than its (seemingly) nonhistorical properties. To take a somewhat unlikely example, we cannot now know that there will not come a time when Beethoven's powerful forms of expression are perceived as mainly offensive (isolated critics of considerable renown have described his music as strident or raucous before). But his place in musical history as one who stretched the expressive power of the classical forms to their limits and helped to form the transition to romanticism is nonetheless perfectly secure. This place cannot now be altered, even though Beethoven was not a father of romanticism when he composed and before others extended the newly forming ideals and strategies into a tradition. We need not speculate about the uncertain artistic future to be confident in this interpretation of his symphonies and their historical significance. Similarly, whether or not twelve-tone compositions ever find real public acceptance (which is becoming more doubtful), and whether they come to be perceived as expressive of various aesthetic qualities (in relation to works as yet to come), they must retain their place in the historical development of music theory and composition.

Real stylistic developments, culminations, deviations, variations, and prophesies allow for relatively stable ascription of historically relative evaluative properties to works and also for stable interpretation of whole works in terms of their historical significance. In both cases recognition of stylistic ideals stabilizes interpretation and evaluation in the face of changing tastes. One can recognize a work as good of its kind, as having properties that fulfill the ideals of a style, even when one does not favor that kind or style of work. Yet more obviously, the historical importance of a work that helped to shape a stylistic tradition that dominated for a substantial period may be secure even when the style is no longer favored. The works of the first romantics retain historical value in periods of antiromantic reaction.

Recognition of artistic ideals implicit in styles need not always require relativizing ascriptions of value-relevant properties to single stylistic movements. Certain ideals initially defined by particular artists or styles continue to be pursued in later styles as well, and comparisons that span movements are therefore fitting. We can say with some confidence, for example, that the ideal of emotional expression in baroque music was in some ways surpassed in the classical and romantic styles but that the ideal of creating intricate and clearly audible counterpoint was not. Such judgments allow for considerable stability in certain interpretations and evaluations that do not relativize aesthetic properties to single styles. The extent of this stability may vary, however, with the probability that future movements will alter the interstylistic standards implicitly invoked. But critics may be able again to judge that probability in light of the degree to which the ideals in question appear to have been fulfilled in the course of art historical development up to their time.

On the level of global interpretation too we thus find neither a single correct historical interpretation of each work nor mere subjective consensus among historians at various times favoring this or that style of historical narrative. Historians, like other interpreters, must explain works as they find them by incorporating them into narratives that describe real stylistic connections and developments. This requirement allows for a variety of interpretations according to historically varying dominant tastes. But once more the operation of taste in the sphere of art history does not nullify the existence of standards for acceptable interpretations. The proper evaluations of artworks and appreciations of their values depend on the availability of acceptable interpretations. But it does not depend on there being just one acceptable interpretation, historical or otherwise, for each work. We may now turn directly to this final topic of evaluation, reiterating at another level our fundamental question whether standards of value in art are a matter of mere taste or whether they can be more objectively grounded.

CHAPTER FIVE

Evaluation

This final chapter will explore the nature of reasons that can support evaluative judgments about artworks. Such judgments range from broad evaluations of whole works to ascriptions of the narrower evaluative properties such as balance or raucousness. I maintained earlier that the latter, though still including evaluative responses of suitable critics, rest on more easily specified objective bases. We are interested here both in the epistemic relation between ascribing the narrower evaluative properties and evaluating artworks as a whole and in how we justify the narrower ascriptions by citing objective or nonevaluative properties of works.

In the second chapter I offered an analysis of aesthetic judgments according to which they are descriptive, expressive, and prescriptive or normative at the same time. These joint features of such judgments suggested a metaphysical account of the evaluative properties they ascribe in terms of relations between objective properties in works and responses of ideal critics or evaluators. The (hypothetical) causal relations at the heart of these properties suggest in turn that the logical or epistemic relations to be spelled out here are inductive, a form of analogical or explanatory inference. We infer from the presence of certain narrowly evaluative or objective properties and the explanations for our reactions to them how ideal critics with similar tastes would react to the same properties in the contexts of the works being evaluated. To justify these judgments to others, we must prompt them to experience the properties to which we are reacting and to make similar (usually implicit) inferences. Hence our critical judgments should direct them to those properties in the works.

In defending this position here, I will also criticize views that hold aesthetic judgments to be justified through deductive arguments or by appeal to aesthetic principles or laws. Once more we will need to reiterate or expand on critical points stated in earlier chapters.

Principles

There are two ways in which we may be led to think that the connection between the ascription of various aesthetic properties to a work and the proper overall evaluation of it is logically stronger than that indicated above. The first is that in which we begin with the ascription of evaluative properties, properties or judgments ascribing them that already include or express evaluative responses. Such positive or negative responses to elements or facets of works, expressed in such terms as delicate, subtle, raucous, or pretentious, enter into and so are closely linked to one's overall response to a work or total evaluation of it. But there are two reasons why the connection between ascription of such properties and overall evaluative judgments is not as strong as it may appear.

First, when we apply such terms only to parts of works, the normally positive response that they express may be completely overridden by the total contexts constituted by other properties in the works. A graceful line, for example, could render an otherwise dynamic work insipid. Second, even when applied to a whole work, a term that normally suggests only positive or only negative evaluation may not express its normal evaluative response. To call a work incoherent or monotonous is normally to indicate a negative appraisal of it. But incoherence can be a virtue in a Lewis Carroll verse or in the theater of the absurd, and likewise for monotony when it is part of the point, as in a Samuel Beckett play or (perhaps) in an Andy Warhol or Frank Stella painting.

Thus, even in the case of ascribing evaluative properties, there can be no entailments or deductive arguments to evaluative judgments of a work as a whole. Nor do such properties *always* contribute in the same way or direction to such evaluations. Conversationally, of course, if a critic ascribes a number of properties that normally contribute only positively to a work's value, and if she notes no normally negative properties, then she need not add that in her opinion the work is a good one. But this conversational implication indicates neither a valid deductive argument nor an appeal to universal aesthetic principles.

The second way in which we may be led to believe in stronger than (weakly) inductive evaluative arguments is by accepting those ideals implicit in the styles of the works being assessed. Whenever we evaluate something as being good or bad *of a kind,* and when the kind implies standards of goodness because of its use in a standard practice or membership in a social institution, then its goodness will seem to be an objective property reducible to other properties of the thing or entailed by their presence. The philosopher's favorite example is a good knife, meaning a sharp and sturdy one good for cutting. In the context of aesthetics, to say that a work is good of its kind is to say that it fulfills the ideals of the style or genre into which the work fits. Here we judge from within an artistic practice or game as the artist played it, asking whether he succeeded in achieving the goals he adopted. In this sense we can recognize a work as good although it does not appeal to our taste. (Another way in which we can do this is by recognizing that we fall short of ideal critics, who would approve of the work.)

If all aesthetic goodness were goodness of a kind in this way, then it might seem that there could be sound deductive arguments leading to evaluative judgments as conclusions. But once again we must recognize that there can be defeaters that disqualify a work containing properties that instantiate the ideals of a given style from being a good example of that style. A symphony in the classical style might be balanced, dramatic, and contain graceful themes and passages. Yet, to revert to an earlier farfetched example, if it contains hyenalike sounds, it is unlikely to be good of its kind. The example is intentionally farfetched to indicate that the list of possible defeaters is open-ended. If it were instead typically limited for particular styles, then we could generate principles and deductive arguments by including clauses or premises specifying the absence of such defeaters.[1] But we cannot specify an open-ended list. Hence there is no entailment from particular properties of works, even evaluative properties, to the goodness of those works even as works of a given kind. The entailment would hold only if a list of properties of a work were to include a stipulation that these were all the evaluatively relevant properties.

A point of greater importance here is that not all aesthetic goodness is goodness in fulfilling the ideals of a particular genre or style. This is a controversial claim. Its defense is closely related to two claims to be defended at some length later in this chapter: that there are value-creating effects of works that are common across genres and that taste can improve, such improvement being marked by changing preferences among genres. If there are common values across styles and genres, and if we can compare the values of different styles or genres (which we can, if we can compare tastes for those types of art), then we can speak of the value of works *tout court*, without considering them only as works of a given kind. And if we can use 'good' in this way as applied to artworks, then this will be its primary or most general sense. Two qualifiers or points of clarification must be added here, however. First, this is not to imply that we can always compare works across very different genres. There may be no answer to the question whether *The Murder of Roger Ackroyd* is better than Vivaldi's Concerto in G Major for Strings and Harpsichord ("Alla Rustica"). It is to imply only that if both of these share value-making properties of many good works, and if these properties are not overridden by negative evaluative properties, then they may be both good works, irrespective of genre. Second, to say that 'good' can be predicated of artworks per se is not to deny that all goodness may be goodness of a kind or goodness in a way.[2] It is to say only that artworks may be good as artworks and not simply as mystery novels or harpsichord concerti.

Our initial conclusion, then, is that there are no laws or sound deductive arguments linking the ascription of particular evaluative aesthetic properties to overall evaluations of works (as works of a given kind or simply as artworks). The justification or defense of the latter evaluations is at least a two-step process, however. The more basic steps involve linking the ascription of broadly evaluative properties to narrower ones and eventually to the perception of objective, nonevaluative properties in the works. But the same argument against strict principles applies at the most basic level as well, as does another that we utilized in arguing against realism in regard to aesthetic properties. The first argument appeals to the relevance of context, the second to different tastes.

Aesthetic principles of the most interesting kind would link objective to evaluative properties in artworks. Strong principles would state sufficient and/or necessary objective conditions for the ascription of evaluative properties. In his seminal article on this topic Sibley argued against there being sufficient conditions of this sort.[3] The straightforward argument from context suffices here. A line of a given shape and color in a painting might have value only there, not in the context of any other painting. If, as maintained earlier, elements within works are transformed by the relations into which they enter, and if these relations are typically nested within broader or higher-order ones, then it is hard to imagine why any part of a work could not be altered in its value or aesthetic effect (the overall evaluative properties to which it contributes) when placed in a different context. Nothing short of a full work and the ways that its various objective properties interact to produce its aesthetic effects guarantees that it has the evaluative properties it does have. Thus no set of objective properties in themselves constitute sufficient conditions for evaluative properties, if it is always possible to embed the former in other broader contexts. Holism may be misguided as a theory of meaning for natural languages but not as a theory of aesthetic value.

In holding nevertheless that (evaluative) aesthetic properties may be "negatively condition governed," Sibley appears to imply that objective properties may constitute necessary conditions for them. If a gaudy work cannot have all pale or dull colors (negative conditions), then bright colors seem to constitute a necessary condition for gaudiness. The claim that there are such necessary conditions has some plausibility, but it is defeated by consideration of context in a different sense. The way that objective properties contribute to evaluative ones is relative to the style in which a work is embedded and to the strategies and constraints (and hence choices among objective properties) available to artists working within that style. In the art deco style, for example, certain colors normally classified as pastels might make a gaudy pattern on the facade of a building, as some of the hotels in South Miami Beach illustrate. The same colors in a painting by Mondrian would certainly not be gaudy. What is relevant here is the range of colors normally used within the respective styles. We cannot therefore say that any objective color properties in themselves are necessary conditions for the aesthetic property.

The example can be generalized. Even if we cannot now imagine certain objective properties contributing to certain evaluative aesthetic ones (for example, sharp and angular lines contributing to gracefulness), it may be that some future style will emerge in which they do so. A standard argument against aesthetic principles is that such rules are always internal to given styles. Thus, even if we talk of only necessary conditions, these can be necessary only for producing evaluative properties in artworks of a given kind. For evaluations of works *tout court*, it is relevant that many great works violate principles stating necessary conditions for evaluative properties in the style then dominant. Such works redefine the tradition and help to create a new style, with new principles of this sort that will in turn be counterexemplified by future great works. Necessary conditions for evaluations of works across styles or genres therefore cannot be stated.

Thus, there are no universal principles from objective to evaluative properties (sufficient conditions) or from evaluative to objective properties (necessary conditions). Some philosophers defend several weaker sorts of connections that I believe to be still too strong. One such supposed relation is the Wittgensteinian criterion. According to criteriologists, critical reasons of the strongest sort, which cite objective properties in support of evaluative judgments, function as criteria for the ascription of evaluative properties.[4] Criteria, in the relevant sense of the concept, are conceptual connections short of entailments but stronger than merely contingent connections. Where x is a criterion for y, it is supposed to be necessary that normally x is y. This allows for defeaters, even open-ended lists of defeaters, but it also holds that x is not merely discovered empirically to be evidence for y. The criterial relation is supposed to hold when we learn to apply the concept of y, learn to call things y's, only on the basis of experiencing x. Then we do not find or discover that y's are x's or x's normally y's. We instead learn this when we learn to apply the concept of y correctly. It is a matter of meaning and is entailed by correct use of language.

The concept of a criterion has been widely utilized in philosophy since Wittgenstein; for example, to express the relation between observed pain behavior and being in pain or between appearing red and being red. The connections here cannot be merely contingent, it is held, because to establish contingent connections we would require an independent way to pick out the states of affairs for which we need the criteria. But we lack such independent means of identification. We cannot pick out red things, for example, except on the basis of how they appear. In aesthetics the notion of a criterion is supposed to capture the relations between, for example, being beautiful and being exquisite, being exquisite and being delicate and graceful, and between the latter and having sweeping but fragile or thin lines (only the last is objective or nonevaluative).

We do not need to analyze such cases in aesthetics specifically to dismiss the position of the criteriologists. I have argued at some length elsewhere that the notion of necessary (but nondeductive) evidence is itself ultimately incoherent.[5] It cannot be the case that *necessarily* that which satisfies the criteria for being F *normally* is F (but may not be because of open-ended defeaters) and therefore is necessarily evidence for F. If it is necessarily true that x normally indicates y, then it must be true in all possible worlds that x normally indicates y. But it cannot be true in all possible worlds that x normally (but not always) indicates y in the sorts of examples given. Conditions that are abnormal (but possible) in our world are not abnormal in all possible worlds. There are possible worlds in which (our) pain behavior typically indicates hilarious delight and in which sweeping, fragile lines in a painting indicate only mawkish sentimentality.

It is true that in our world we pick out what we call red things only on the basis of their normally appearing red. But there are possible worlds in which we cannot coherently ascribe colors to objects themselves on the basis of how they appear (suppose objects appear different shades to normal observers or are known to change their pigments when not being observed by humans). Thus apparent colors cannot *necessarily* be evidence for colors of objects themselves. More generally, if it is only normally the case (in our world) that x indicates y, then x cannot necessarily indicate y, even if it is the case that we learn to pick out (what we assume to be) y's on the basis of observing x. Once we learn to recognize defeaters and admit that the list of them is open-ended, we also must admit that the relation in question is contingent. (In the usual examples it is causal in some sense. When this is the case, we can infer a cause as the best explanation for what we observe without an independent way of picking out the cause.)

The criteriologist is on even weaker ground in the aesthetics cases. First, it is doubtful that we learn to pick out graceful objects, for example, on the basis of such limited and specific properties as thin, sweeping lines. We learn the property on the basis of paradigm complex objects that might include Willie Mays or Chris Evert, or a swan or Mozart aria, as well as a Brancusi sculpture or Botticelli painting. The former two give us the suggestion of fluid motion and efficient ease, and the latter two may as well, but they do so in very different ways, since the latter two do not move at all. Second, in the case of objective and evaluative aesthetic properties even in the same object, the former will indicate the latter only to those who share the taste of the person ascribing the properties. A painting with gently curving lines may be graceful to one critic and insipid to another. The argument from taste that defeated both realism for evaluative properties and the relation of supervenience between objective and evaluative properties also shows from an epistemological point of view that objective properties cannot be criteria for evaluative qualities.

This argument works along with the argument from context to defeat yet weaker proposed principles as well. We saw earlier that the same objective properties do not *always* count in the same way toward the instantiation of the same evaluative properties; all depends on the context in which the former are embedded. Differences in taste even among ideal critics shows that objective properties do not *only* count in one direction (Sibley thought that they do). Even the same lines in the same work do not count only positively toward gracefulness; they may count negatively toward insipidness for other critics. We therefore cannot even have principles of the following form: Whatever has objective property F is prima facie G (evaluative property). The concept of 'prima facie' here, or of F's being a G-making property, requires that F count in only one direction toward the realization of G.

There may seem to be a difference in this regard in the two levels of justification we have been discussing. If we ascribe an evaluative property to a work as a whole, it certainly seems that this may be linked to an overall evaluation of the work by a principle of this weak kind. To call a work powerful is certainly normally to suggest that it is a good work; to call it incoherent is normally to suggest the opposite. Can we then say that in so far as it is powerful it is to that extent (prima facie) good? No. We saw above that even such terms do not always or only have their usual evaluative force when applied to certain (avant-garde) works. A powerful work may move us only to disgust, and although some critics might judge it good on that ground, others might not. We cannot say here that for the latter critics its being powerful is overridden by its being disgusting, for it may be powerful only in virtue of its repulsiveness. It is equally obvious in the case of the theater of the absurd that plays in this style may not be bad in so far as they are incoherent; if anything, incoherence can be a good-making property in such works.

Thus, even the usual kind of weak inductive principle linking properties in artworks themselves to evaluative properties and overall evaluations fails. The impossibility of stating such principles is well illustrated by recent attempts of aestheticians to do so. We may consider first a single example from David Pole. He proposes as a case of a nonevaluative description that entails a (prima facie) evaluation a character without apparent motive inserted into a play for the sole purpose of moving the plot along.[6] The lack of motive here is a defect, and necessarily so, Pole maintains. He recognizes, of course, that this feature counts in only a prima facie way toward a negative evaluation of the play, as is obvious from the fact that his example is from a well-known play by Shakespeare. But the problem is instead that the generalization is not perfect. In a play such as Beckett's *Waiting for Godot*, lack of motive may be a virtue insofar as it is part of the point. This is not to say that all critics must approve of that play, but insofar as they do, they will be unlikely to disapprove of the lack of apparent motives in the characters. Nor can we find a non–question-begging relevant difference between these plays that accounts for the different effects of this feature and that we can generalize. All we can say is that *Godot* is not the sort of play in which lack of motives counts negatively. Clearly that sort of statement will not do as a way to save a principle.

The failure of Pole's principle can be explained by either or both features of aesthetic qualities to which I have drawn attention (that they are transformed by the relations into which they enter and that the same objective bases elicit different responses from ideal critics). The lack of motive that may be a defect in the context of one play is not a defect when related to other elements in a different play. Both of these plays, but certainly *Godot*, may elicit approval from some critics and disapproval from others. Such differences will transfer to this particular feature of the play as well.

The most important and best-known recent attempt to state weak, inductive aesthetic principles is Monroe Beardsley's theory of aesthetic value. Perhaps recognizing the force of the argument from context, he proposed such principles only for higher-order properties of whole artworks. According to him, there are three such properties that always contribute only positively to the value of works: unity, complexity, and intensity. Other properties have aesthetic value insofar as they contribute to these higher-order properties of whole works. Beardsley holds that a work is never

good because it lacks unity or is disorganized, for example. Nor can
it be bad because it is unified. Such principles are inductive and
state only tendencies, however. A unified work is not always good
overall, but a work with any of these properties tends to cause valuable aesthetic experience in its audience.

In assessing this set of proposed principles, we should first note
several ambiguities in the use of these three terms. First, each of
them can be used either nonevaluatively or evaluatively, to indicate
objective properties in works themselves or to include positive responses to them. If a critic is using one of these terms evaluatively,
then she would use a different term to refer to the same objective
property if she did not approve of its presence in the work, for example, 'repetitious' or 'monotonous' instead of 'unified'. Second,
Beardsley sometimes uses these terms to refer to qualities within
experience itself, qualities that cause or indicate the full engagement
of a subject with a work.[7] More typically, however, he uses them to
refer to qualities of works that cause experiences of this sort, and it
is this use that enters into the thesis of aesthetic principles.[8]

The arguments against aesthetic principles stated earlier in this
section apply in obvious ways to Beardsley's theory. When the
three properties he specifies are themselves evaluative, they may
nevertheless conflict with one another or interact negatively in the
contexts of particular works. In fact, unity and intensity seem to
tend to be at odds with complexity. On the one hand, these relations
give Beardsley a way to avoid seeming counterexamples. If a critic
praises a work for variety, simplicity, or delicate subtlety, this may
seem to contradict Beardsley's claim that works cannot be good for
lack of unity, complexity, or intensity. But he can reply that variety
here is not a lack of unity but is a form of complexity; simplicity as
conceived by this critic is not lack of complexity but a kind of unity;
and subtlety is not lack of intensity but another form of complexity.
On the other hand, the only reason these replies are available is that
an increase in complexity is normally a decrease in unity and/or intensity. Beardsley can, of course, claim that increases in unity are always good only given the same degree of complexity, and vice versa.
(Hutcheson said something very much like this.) But these would
be far more restricted principles than those suggested above.

This claim itself will not hold up for the more interesting sort of
principle that links objective or nonevaluative properties to aesthetic value. As indicated above, the same property in a work that

one critic calls unity another will call monotony. What is complex to one is disorganized or muddled or baffling to another, and what is intense to one is strident or raucous to another. Critics might not praise a work for being disorganized, since that term normally has a negative connotation, but they might approvingly refer to the same objective formal properties as being spontaneous, bold, or disdainful of rigid formalism. A work may be intensely ugly in a complex variety of ways that all contribute to a unified effect, that of ugliness. And whereas some critics may approve of such complex but unified intensity, others will not.

Beardsley's theory, hearkening back to Hutcheson's, is, of course, not without considerable plausibility. In earlier describing and praising the aesthetic potentiality of sonata-allegro form in symphonic music, I extolled its ability to guide the listener through complex relations, creating, through its repetitions and standardized structure, unity within complexity and increasing intensity by allowing the listener to experience the musical developments affectively. When elements of works in this form are perceived as fitting (unity) the complex pattern that challenges one's perceptual cognition, so as to allow for maximal interaction among these elements, the result can be an intensely rich and therefore rewarding or pleasurable experience. When Beardsley's three properties are ascribed to such experience itself, they signal the same sort of aesthetically valuable consciousness that we find described in somewhat other terms in the theories of Kant and Dewey. I agree with all these theories that aesthetic value lies in a work's producing experience of this sort. What I deny is that we can specify how artworks are to do this for all audiences and what objective properties within them will always produce this kind of response or even tend to do so. Beardsley's idea that (nonevaluative) properties within works simply mirror the same properties within aesthetic experience, and therefore can be neutrally described in exactly the same terms, is both simplistic and too artistically limiting. Music that is unified, complex, and intense (many twelve-tone pieces qualify, for example) may sound awful and may completely fail to engage us, whereas paintings that appear very simple can attract and absorb our full attention for extended periods.

There is one yet weaker sort of proposed aesthetic principle that remains to be considered. Fully cognizant of the argument from context, George Dickie proposes that certain properties (Beardsley's

and certain others) *in isolation from others* always contribute in
only one direction toward proper evaluations of works.[9] Unfortunately, this proposal makes little sense, if, as I have suggested, artworks derive their aesthetic value mainly from the ways their objective properties interact. We have little if any idea how to conceive
of a painting with multiple properties as if it had only one. Even
simple paintings will have degrees of several of the higher-order
properties mentioned in Beardsley's theory. Where one such property dominates completely (say, formal unity with no expressive intensity or representational, or symbolic, complexity), the result is
usually only an impoverished aesthetic experience. Nor does
Dickie's proposal do anything to counter the argument from taste.
Even if we could consider aesthetic properties in isolation, it still
seems that objective properties valued by one critic might not be
valued by another. Finally, there would be little point in considering aesthetic properties in isolation, even if we could develop principles from doing so, if these properties are always transformed, often unpredictably, by the relations into which they enter in the
aesthetic contexts in which they are actually found.

I conclude that there are no principles linking objective to evaluative properties or particular evaluative properties to overall evaluations. But if we cannot generalize the reasons for our aesthetic
judgments, then how can they function as genuine reasons? How
can the reasons for which I make a judgment, even if I articulate
them, have any force for you? If no generalization at all were possible, then reasons could not have any interpersonal force. But the
absence of principles does not imply that no generalization is possible. If I try to influence your evaluative judgment of a work by
specifying the reasons for mine (by pointing ultimately to objective
properties in the work), I imply that an ideal critic who shares my
general taste would react to these qualities in the same way and that
you therefore ought to do so as well. The generalization, as Kant
held, is from my reaction to a particular work to the reactions of
others, not from this work to other works. But Kant exaggerated
the universality of such judgments. They must be relativized to
tastes. One's interest in the judgments and reasons of any particular
critic depends in part on the degree to which his taste is shared
(only in part, since the specification of reasons by reference to
properties in a work can still guide fresh perceptions of the work in
the absence of shared taste).

We can also generalize, despite the lack of principles, on the ways that great artworks affect us. (It is from such common effects in experience that Beardsley's theory gains the plausibility it has.) To offer reasons for evaluative judgments is to predict how the works in question will inform the experience of ideal critics so as to prompt like evaluations from them. We can study and explain these effects, thereby developing a theory of aesthetic value, without being able to provide formulas for creating great works, formulas that principles of the kind denied here would comprise.

Comparison to Moral Judgment

We may further elucidate the character of aesthetic judgments and the evaluative properties to which they refer by comparing them to moral judgments and moral properties. Both the similarities and the differences are revealing and need to be discussed in turn.

The most relevant similarity lies in the structures of (evaluative) aesthetic properties and moral properties and in the accounts that therefore can be offered of judgments ascribing these properties. To say that an object has an evaluative aesthetic property is, we held, to say that an ideal critic would respond in a certain way based on perception of more basic aesthetic properties. Similarly, ascribing a moral property such as rightness to an action can be analyzed as saying that the action is such as to elicit a certain response (e.g., approval) from an ideal judge by virtue of its more basic moral properties. These analyses reflect the simultaneous expressive, normative, and objective facets of evaluative judgments in both domains. In both cases we can ascribe more broadly evaluative or objectively specific properties and offer chains of justification moving from the former to the latter. An action's being wrong, for example, may consist in its being contemptible, cruel, or murderous. The narrower properties may again be viewed as relational, the first involving a particular affective or emotional component and the other two including specific sorts of objective properties or relations.

A second important similarity lies in the need to relativize the truth of evaluative judgments in the two domains to groups of ideal evaluators. In the case of rightness, there are incompatible ways (for example, strongly rights-oriented versus collectivist or loyalist versus impartialist) of resolving those conflicts among interests that give rise to moral debate. These conflicting general moral frameworks may be acceptable to different ideal judges, evaluators who qualify as ideal under any non–question-begging specification of relevant qualifications. What is right within one such framework (for example, redistributive taxation) may not be right within another, just as an aesthetically good work for one critic may not be for another.[10] Thus, to say that an action is right is to say that it would be approved by an ideal judge who shares one's moral framework, an obvious parallel to the appeal to shared taste in the analysis of aesthetic judgment.[11]

Differences between the two domains begin to emerge when we consider the nature of the base properties (those objective features of artworks or actions that are aesthetically or morally relevant) and the characteristics of ideal evaluators that make them ideal. Although we required a complex disjunctive list of base properties that typically contribute to the aesthetic value of artworks, we can characterize morally relevant properties simply as those features of agents' actions that importantly affect the interests of others. Regarding the qualities of ideal evaluators, such critics of artworks must be knowledgeable, unbiased, sensitive, and of developed taste. Some characteristics of ideal moral judges are similar. They must be impartial and sympathetic, as aesthetic judges must be unbiased and sensitive, although impartiality in the moral sphere is both more central and more variable (to moral framework).

The main difference in these characterizations is that whereas aesthetic critics must be knowledgeable of the styles or types of artworks being judged and of the historical contexts into which they fit, moral judges, in addition to knowing the relevant nonmoral features of the actions being judged, must be rational or coherent in their sets of moral judgments. The latter characteristic indicates a basic difference in the constraints under which ideal evaluators in the two domains operate. Many philosophers since Kant would describe this difference by saying that moral judgments must conform to principles whereas aesthetic judgments do not.[12] According to this view, the demand for coherence that constrains moral but not aesthetic judgments is met when we can state universal rules under which our particular judgments fit. But this view is mistaken. Although there is a difference of this kind between judgments in the two domains, it does not lie in the existence of universal principles linking nonmoral with moral properties.

It is clear upon reflection that no ordinary nonevaluative properties are sufficient for the correct application of 'right' and 'wrong'. There may be sufficient properties, but these will be narrower moral properties. Murder, for example, may always be wrong, but the class of murders is not determined by a set of nonmoral properties. Murders are morally (or legally, if we are speaking of legal wrongness) unjustified homicides, those lacking reasons acceptable to ideal judges. (What one moral system judges murder, another might accept as justifiable homicide.) Lying, by contrast, may be reducible to nonmoral terms (speaking falsely with intent to deceive), but then a statement's being a lie is never sufficient in itself to show that it is wrong to utter it.

Kant's moral criterion, in its application to perfect duties, may seem to be an exception. Isn't the fact that one could not will an action universally sufficient to show that the action is wrong? This is certainly not the place for full treatment of this question, but consideration of an example from Kant himself indicates why he has not isolated a sufficient *nonmoral* condition for wrongness. Consider willing the universal breaking of promises for mere convenience. Whether a promise is considered broken merely for convenience or for some more weighty or justificatory reason involves the moral perceptions of properly qualified and situated evaluators and hence is not reducible to nonmoral conditions. More generally, subjective principles of action to be willed universally must include reference to relevant circumstances, and what is considered relevant is a matter of moral evaluation, a matter that may again differ from one moral framework to another.

As in aesthetics, it is not possible to make nonmoral properties sufficient for moral judgment by building in all exceptions in advance, since exceptions will be open-ended. As in aesthetics, once we admit the absence of sufficient nonevaluative properties, it is a short step to deny the existence of principles stating prima facie conditions. If we admit, for example, that it is generally wrong not to lie in order to save an innocent life, then it serves no purpose (other than to save an implausible theory) to say that lying to save a life is prima facie or, insofar as it is a lie, wrong. Other instances of intentional deception—for example, in regard to one's health or state of mind when answering the question "How are you?"—seem more obviously completely blameless. These are not instances of a

prima facie wrong being overridden by more powerful considerations. Even killing a person, which is almost always wrong, is not
always almost wrong. Why should we have to say that killing
Hitler in 1941 would have been, insofar as it was killing, to that extent (prima facie) wrong (unless we are under the spell of this theory)? In my view it would have been once more *completely* blameless.

Thus we have found one similarity and one difference between
aesthetics and ethics in regard to principles. The similarity lies in
the absence in both domains of principles linking nonevaluative to
evaluative properties. The difference lies in the fact that we do find
some principles in ethics, but not in aesthetics, linking narrower
evaluative properties to overall evaluations. We noted above that
murder is always wrong, whereas we could not make similar statements about artworks always being good if they have certain narrower evaluative properties. Similarly, having courage may always
be a virtue, although a courageous killer is more dangerous than a
cowardly one, and, more important, the same actions that make one
courageous in the eyes of some may make one only foolhardy or
cold-blooded in the eyes of others. In aesthetics, remember, we
could not even say that being powerful, for example, is always an
artistic virtue of a work. This difference may be explained by
deeper features of evaluative properties and by the functions of
norms and discourse in the two domains. Before seeking that explanation, we should return to the difference in constraints on the two
sorts of judgments, which we have not yet indicated and which will
point us toward the same deeper account.

Although we cannot exhaustively state in advance the nonmoral
grounds for moral evaluations, we must find some morally relevant
(nonmoral) difference each time we judge differently two cases that
seem otherwise similar. Although it is not possible to state nonmoral properties that are sufficient for homicides to count as murders, for example, it is possible to state a nonmoral ground that differentiates each case of justified homicide (as it arises) from cases of
murder. Such differences must be considered to count generally, in
other cases if not in all (that the victim has red hair, for example, is
thereby ruled irrelevant). We cannot make an exception by differentiating one case from another that is otherwise similar unless we
are willing to accept the consequences of the differentiating feature
making a difference in other cases. If such a generally relevant dif-

ference cannot be found between two cases, then they must be considered analogous and judged morally the same. It can then be argued that the truth of a moral judgment consists in its being analogous to some settled judgment and in its denial being differentiable, making it a member of some maximally coherent set. A maximally coherent set is one in which, for all differences in judgments, we can specify nonmoral differences that count generally.[13]

This is again not the place to defend this metaethical view.[14] The point is instead to indicate the absence of this crucial constraint in the domain of aesthetic judgment. This difference is as important as the lack of principles that characterizes both realms of discourse. In aesthetics there is no requirement to judge artworks similarly when no generally relevant nonaesthetic difference between them can be found. Differences between works can be relevant to aesthetic evaluation without being generalizable. We judge, for example, that Mozart or one of his symphonies is better than Salieri or one of his symphonies, and if asked for a reason, we might well respond that Mozart's music is less predictable than Salieri's. But this response does not commit us to the view that being less predictable is generally a musical virtue. That Schönberg's music is less predictable (auditorily) than Mozart's does not at all contribute toward Schönberg's being a better composer. (And many other composers as well are less predictable than Mozart without being in the least better than him for it).

This crucial difference between the two domains also can be explained by the different functions of discourse within them and by the resultant difference in what counts as a relevant property. First, since vital interests of different persons are affected by moral decisions, it is important how these decisions are arrived at and how disagreements are settled, whether rationally or by force. Aesthetic disagreements do not involve so broad and direct conflicts among important interests. It is therefore not as crucial that they be resolved by argument of the sort that the requirement for coherence in ethics makes possible. Differences in taste are more easily tolerated. Aesthetic disagreements are settled, if at all, not by analogical argument but by pointing to unnoticed features of works and awaiting an anticipated common response.

Second, moral norms exist mainly to prohibit and prevent only those actions and situations that destroy peaceful, cooperative relations within and among groups, leaving individuals free to do as they please where such norms do not apply. These norms therefore need to be limited and straightforward in their application. Given this function and this requirement, it is predictable that what is considered a morally relevant property will be limited and that there will be categories like murder that always indicate wrong or prohibited actions. Given these limits on what is to count as a morally relevant property, it is possible to require that such relevance must be generalizable to other situations. This is possible because the probability of defeaters may be relatively low, despite our not being able to list all possible defeaters for particular properties in advance. Artworks, in contrast, are made to engage us as fully as possible, and therefore we may expect that many of their observable properties will be aesthetically relevant. And we do indeed find that small changes in formal relations change the evaluative properties of artworks in major and often unpredictable ways. Generalization of aesthetically relevant properties is not possible because the number of potential defeaters seems boundless.

If the semantic status of aesthetic judgments differs from that of moral judgments on coherentist grounds, it also differs on the other side from that of expressions of pure personal preference, as in taste for foods. Critics of artworks do provide reasons for their evaluations, and they thereby suggest that others ought to share their judgments. This suggestion need not be viewed as bald prescription. Reasons, however, rarely appeal to other artworks for confirmation by analogy (at least not in the presence of a work itself). Instead, they consist in features of the work itself that would move or engage ideal critics of certain taste. Unlike paradigm moral cases, paradigm artworks of value do not function as settled cases to which other works must be analogous in their objective properties. Instead, agreement on a set of paradigms establishes a reference class of critics who share taste, so as to suggest that disagreement beyond this set might indicate failure to satisfy ideal conditions for evaluation.

The assimilation of aesthetics to ethics in value theory is a two-sided mistake. When morality is aestheticized, the idea is usually that agents have an immediate grasp of what is right, even in the most complex situations involving conflicts among interests. We are to trust our feeling or moral sense, which is supposed to be akin to our immediate grasp of beauty in objects. This again is doubly wrong. Aesthetic appreciation may require much training and knowledge. And our moral feelings are likely to be misled by su-

perficial similarities in appearances, as when our reaction to the
physical appearance of a fetus causes us to oppose abortion without
thinking of the morally relevant properties of fetuses and infants.

When aesthetics is assimilated to morality, the idea is usually that
there must be laws governing aesthetic judgments, even though no
one has been able to state any. There also may be emphasis, as in
Kant, on the extent to which both sorts of judgments must be impartial, sensitive, freely made, and universal. The first claim is doubly mistaken, since, as argued above, there are no principles linking
nonevaluative to evaluative properties in either domain. The second
exaggerates the generality that is possible in these judgments, the
extent to which all moral judgments must be impartial (or all sensitive to the same set of morally relevant differences), and the centrality of impartiality (or disinterest) in aesthetic judgment.

The most important similarity between the domains (for our
purposes) lies, I have claimed, in the structure of evaluative properties in both. The most important difference lies in the coherentist
constraint that governs moral judgment and reasoning but does not
apply in aesthetics. This difference, explained by the different functions of discourse in the two realms, should make us wary of in-
flated claims regarding the power of art to educate us morally or
make us better moral judges. These claims have been made for various arts, and their plausibility varies with the art form invoked.
Music, I argued earlier, does affect and arouse our emotions, and so
it can have interesting psychological effects. But the idea, intermit-
tently advanced since Plato, that musical harmony and grace can
make us persons of moral harmony and grace finds little empirical
support. For every Verdi there is a Wagner. Literature, of course,
can be of use in moral education by introducing us to new types of
characters and situations and allowing us to imaginatively try out
different roles. Experience with fiction, like experience in real life,
can refine or blunt our moral sensibilities. But even here, the claim
that an appreciation of literature is necessary for a full moral education, that *only* literary narrative can sensitize us to the dense, fine-
grained structure of morally charged situations,[15] exaggerates the
extent to which morally charged situations are so fine-grained in
their relevant properties. As argued above, the (Hobbesian) view of
morality as a set of institutionalized norms for preventing behavior
destructive of peaceful and cooperative relations and endeavors
suggests otherwise.

Valuable Effects

So far in this chapter I have been emphasizing the impossibility of certain kinds of generalizations in aesthetics. We may now turn to the sort of generalization across the arts that is possible. I have argued that although we cannot find principles linking objective properties in works to their effects on us and our subsequent evaluative responses, we can generalize about the sorts of effects that works we praise highly have on us. The latter claim may seem implausible. Aside from the fact that great works all attract and hold our interest, it may seem that their effects are quite diverse. Some cheer us up, others depress; some spur us to political action, others afford us a feeling of calm and well-being; and so on.

One clue that there nevertheless is a common sort of effect among fine works is my earlier claim that we cannot understand the values of such separate sources of value as representation and expression unless we take account of the ways they interact so as to contribute to the total experience of the works. These interactions, in which, for example, sensuous qualities are modified by formal relations and representation and form determines what is represented and is enriched by representation and expressive qualities on higher levels, create rich layers of relations among elements within works. The perception of these elements that are thereby imbued with structure, feeling, and content is thus rendered intensely meaningful, as each is related to others in these ways and perceived as such. The value of such works lies first in the challenge and richness of the perceptual, affective, and cognitive experience they afford. Symbolic and expressive density combines here with sensuous feel.

From the subjective side, all one's perceptual, cognitive, and affective capacities can be engaged in apprehending these relations, even if one's grasp of them is imperfect or only implicit. These different facets of appreciation are not only engaged simultaneously but are also often indissolubly united, as when formal relations among musical tones or painted shapes are experienced as felt tensions and resolutions and perhaps as higher-order or more ordinary emotions as well. Our grasp of the complex historical relations into which a work fits and of its referential or symbolic content also informs the ways we perceive it. The understanding that results from this cognitive input, the answer to the challenge that many works present to understanding, is another source of satisfaction to be derived from their appreciation. Finally, we may be, as it were, practically engaged in the active perception of a work if we have the expertise to identify with the pursuit of musical or artistic goals that are defined by the unfolding of the work or by the artist in relation to his tradition. The core concept of appreciation as the proper subjective activity or attitude toward a fine work captures this union of sensory, cognitive, affective, and volitional components.

When we are so fully and satisfyingly involved in appreciating an artwork, we can be said to lose our ordinary, practically oriented selves in the world of the work. This central metaphor of a work as a world applies first perhaps in the realm of literature, where this world can be identified with the set of propositions that are fictionally true in the work. It is a natural complement also to the thesis that art imitates reality, thus constituting a secondary realm apart from it. But I intend the notion of art and the artwork as an alternative world more broadly, to divorce it from the theory of mimesis (imitation) and even from the fact that many artworks refer externally in some way. As I am using this notion, it refers primarily to the object of our full and completely absorbed engagement. In this sense a piece of nonrepresentational instrumental music can engage us so fully as to constitute another world for us, at least temporarily. Given the ability of the best artworks to capture us in this way, there are other reasons as well beyond the usual ones to think of them as alternative worlds.

They contain space and time, for example, but not the space and time of the real world. As noted previously, musical notes are (metaphorically) spatially related and music therefore moves through time, but this space and time are ideal rather than real.[16] We also noted how such time is condensed (in relation to real or lived time) in that emotional changes expressed in music occur far more rapidly than in real life, allowing us to experience or perceive a full gamut of varying or opposed emotions in the course of a single piece (normally no more than an hour in real time). In reading literature we can vicariously experience lifetimes in a matter of hours.

Similarly, within the borders of a painting's frame may be revealed vast and deep spaces, space that is clearly otherworldly in relation to the real flat surface of the canvas. (There is a tension in this respect in regard to the size of paintings. The space within the borders of smaller canvases is more condensed, so they may be experienced more intensely. Yet they also have a tendency to become objects for us in the real world. Larger canvases envelop our perception in their spaces more easily, but these spaces tend to be less condensed.) Time is frozen in paintings, yet narrative or historical pictures may incorporate both past and future into their present action, sometimes literally in that characters or actions from different times may appear in the same spaces, more commonly in that present action or broader themes cannot be understood without reference to past and future. This condensation of space and time in the worlds of artworks contributes to their felt intensity, which helps to explain or reinforce our deep engagements with them.[17]

   A third reason for thinking of works as alternative worlds is that although, as noted, we may (and if trained typically do) become caught up in pursuing the goals they define for our ongoing experience of them, such pursuits take us completely away from our ordinary pursuits in the real world. Other recreational activities besides the appreciation of artworks engage our mental (including perceptual and affective) capacities fully, for example, sports at a sufficiently involved and high level. But in sports we physically act in physical space and time in pursuit of real goals fixed by the rules. In appreciating art we are comparatively inactive in the real world, sitting still in a darkened theater or concert hall, standing still before a painting. We isolate ourselves from physical activities in the real world in order to enter the alternative worlds of artworks.

   The thesis that artworks provide us alternative worlds as objects of our complete engagement throws light on some earlier disputes in aesthetics. One is the debate over whether aesthetic appreciation requires "psychical distance," whether we must remain emotionally detached (to a certain degree) to appreciate artworks fully. Both sides to this dispute turn out to be partially right. Appreciation of art as art requires distancing oneself from the immediate practical world (although understanding the moral or political dimensions of works requires knowledge of those realms in the real world). Likewise, if we are to treat a real object or scene as an object of aesthetic appreciation, we must distance ourselves from its ordinary causal nexus that determines our usual practical concerns with it. But when confronting an artwork and not an ordinary object or scene, our becoming distanced from the world of our everyday concerns is accomplished through our being fully occupied with grasping the internal and external relations of the elements of the work at various levels. The artwork as artwork is detached from our ordinary world (although part of its point is often to reflect on that world by comparison), but only when we as viewers are least detached from the work.

I have claimed that the proposed thesis also explains more particular values of artworks that cannot be explained in isolation. One virtue of works not previously mentioned upon which light can now be thrown is that of originality. According to the present thesis, this value is genuine but also derivative and secondary. A work must first engage our cognitive and affective capacities through the interaction of its aesthetic qualities at various levels before it can be said to constitute an alternative world. Unless it does so, the fact that it is new or original counts for nothing in itself. But originality in a work that does so engage us on other grounds makes the world of the work truly alternative to other worlds encountered, and a different world can be further engaging on that score. Hence originality is of value when a work is valuable on other grounds, otherwise not.

The thesis also explains the conflicting attitudes of different philosophers toward art in general, both those who underestimate its value and those who overestimate its importance or centrality among human endeavors. Art as the provider of alternative worlds might naturally be opposed by philosophers who think they can provide direct knowledge of a perfect state for humans in this world. For them alternatives can only distract us from the task of realizing that state. Hence Plato's attitude toward art as a frivolous but enticing distraction from true knowledge and Hegel's somewhat similar view of art as an inferior (if historically necessary) sort of knowledge. On the other side, those idealists such as Nietzsche who see the real world and any science of it as an artistic creation (albeit grown stale and fossilized) view truly original art as the highest human endeavor, indeed the only one worthy of the name. This not only constitutes a bad explanation for our experience of the real world but also reduces the otherness of artworks that, according to the present thesis, explains much of the value they have.

Some philosophers might object that any theory that distances art from the real world disenfranchises it, seeks by this move to render it practically or politically innocuous.[18] The theory I am de-

fending does not deny, however, that art can have political effect or
that this aim motivates some works of high merit. It holds only that
such effects of great works are indirect, by means of their creating
alternative worlds in which we are fully engaged while experiencing
them, and that the latter effects are common across good works that
are politically motivated and those that are not. If, in a repressive
society, artworks present the only views of alternative worlds, they
can be a most important impetus for change and the chief danger to
the regime in power. But it is the repression itself that creates the
danger and gives to artworks this role played by more direct political expression elsewhere. Artworks with political content can also
be effective in motivating those who normally remain politically
unmotivated precisely because of the ways the works otherwise engage us.

In a context of free expression in a society like ours, artworks are
naturally given even greater freedom than other forms of expression. This is explicable if artistic expression belongs to or seems to
belong to another world and therefore is capable of only indirect
effects in this one. That this is so explains why the question of aesthetic value arises when censorship of offensive expression is being
considered. It is not simply a matter of balancing hedonistic value
(aesthetic pleasure) against disvalue (offense) but of introducing a
different kind of value, easily metaphorized as arising from or belonging to another world. This distancing of offensive material in
true art renders it more tolerable, which is not to deny that some
forms of expression are offensive wherever they occur.

It is also natural and justifiable that the state, which so much determines our real social environment, should subsidize the provision of alternative environments (although the justification will depend partly upon the costs). This argument for public subsidy of
the arts differs in kind from that which appeals to the decoration of
public space so as to improve the quality of life for those who occupy it and differs even from that which appeals to the expression
of a common creative life in the community in that the latter are
more easily weighed (and outweighed) against more pressing social
needs. The value of producing objects that can engage our full be-
ings, of providing alternative worlds that we can occupy however
briefly, is not fully commensurable with that of meeting needs in
the real social environment (which is again not to say that people
should starve so that art may be produced).

The former is not hard to specify further once it is granted that this is a value central and common to artworks across their different media. Full engagement in another world as the object of such complete attention offers an often welcome escape from one's affairs in this world and from one's practically occupied self as well. One escapes from natural and social worlds to which we are at best satisficingly adapted into worlds designed to challenge and satisfy, from which all extraneous noise has been excluded. The effect of escape to another world is heightened by the various devices that separate the artwork and make it self-enclosed: picture frames, the framing of symphonic pieces by tonic sections, beginnings and endings in literary works, museums, concert halls, darkened theaters, all those venues bemoaned by aestheticians mysteriously nostalgic for an age before fine art was fine art. (According to the present thesis the museum is not so different from the church and cathedral, which it often replaced as the portal to other worlds through artworks.) The effect of losing one's self can be lessened if one imagines oneself in the world of a work (which is then imagined to be one's ordinary world). Hence the present thesis disagrees with those theories that view such imagining as typical of aesthetic appreciation.[19]

Artworks as other worlds may also reflect by comparison on this one, revealing possibilities for actions, ways of perceiving, or transformations of real social structures. The more abstract the work, however, the more abstract and general, and often more difficult and speculative, are the comparisons in these regards. Abstract painters such as Mondrian as well as philosophers of music have made exalted claims regarding the power of abstract works to reveal possibilities for and motivate the production of harmonious relations everywhere in the real world, especially in the social realm.[20] But there is little or no evidence that abstract works have ever had such effects. Thus this value is less universal across media and styles than is the value of entering other worlds for its own sake and for its refreshing effects on a person's own faculties.

We may test this thesis regarding the central and shared value of fine artworks not only by its explanatory power but also against examples and seeming counterexamples. Perhaps the cases most congenial to the thesis come from my own favorite art form, opera. As just one example, consider Leonora's famous opening aria from the second scene of the final act of Verdi's *La Forza del Destino* (see

Figure 5.1). The scene takes place by the hermit's cave near the monastery where she has been secluded since fleeing her brother after her lover had killed her father. The surging and ominous destiny theme that pursues her through the opera (providing some unity to a rambling, epic-type plot) introduces the aria. The first notes of the vocal line and its first word, '*Pace*' (peace), contrast with this theme. This vocal melody hearkens back for some critics to Schubert's "Ave Maria," expressing an equally haunting and resigned sadness. It is accompanied mainly by a harp arpeggio, reinforcing Leonora's plea for the peace that eludes her and reminding other critics of Bellini. The vocal line rises with her memory of Alvaro, her lover. The destiny theme again breaks into the accompaniment without breaking the melodic line, the accompaniment consisting otherwise of various instruments delicately blended and moving mainly between G minor and B-flat minor. The expected calm ending to the aria never arrives, as a tremolo in the orchestra announces intruders and changes the mood suddenly to stark fear. Here we have a reminder of past violence and a premonition of that to come. Indeed, the dramatic action and music then build relentlessly to their climax in the stabbing of Leonora, punctuated at that point by a furious, dissonant pounding in the orchestra that brings all movement in both action and music to an abrupt halt.

We may take note here of all the significant relations that must be grasped in appreciating this aria. First, as in any musical piece, there are the internal relations among motifs and harmonic movements that constitute its musical structure as well as the ways these motifs and harmonies in themselves express emotions and (less often) represent. Second, there are relations of melodic vocal line to text and of accompaniment to both, the instruments sometimes carrying separate melodic lines as well. (Here the harp accompaniment reinforces the plea for peace and the destiny theme contrasts with it while expressing the deeper underlying mood and metaphysical reality.) Third, there is the relation of all of this to the ongoing action, and of all of this plus the present action to prior and ensuing action. In the larger structure of the work, the present music connects to earlier passages (the repetition of the destiny theme) and to later passages (the foreshadowing of the orchestra tremolo), paralleling relations among the actions in the drama. The music relates to musical precedents (Schubert and Bellini) and perhaps to later styles (in the dissonant passages, for example). This aria relates to other

MELODIA

ENE VI: Valley among inaccessible rocks, traversed by a stream. At rear, on the spectator's left is a grotto with practicable entrance; above it is a bell, which can be rung from inside. It is sunset. The scene darkens slowly; the moon comes out, shining brilliantly. Dona Leonora, pale and worn, emerges from the grotto, in agitation.

SCENA VI. Valle fra rupi inaccessibili, attraversata da un ruscello. Nel fondo, a sinistra dello spettatore, è una grotta con porta praticabile, e sopra una campana che si potrà suonare dall'interno. È il tramonto. La scena si oscura lentamente; la luna apparisce splendidissima.

Donna Leonora pallida, sfigurata, esce dalla grotta agitatissima.

FIGURE 5.1 Musical score from Verdi's *La Forza del Destino*, Scene VI. Published by Edwin Kalmus, New York, 1968. Reprinted with permission.

158

FIGURE 5.1 *(continued)*

FIGURE 5.1 *(continued)*

162

FIGURE 5.1   *(continued)*

Verdi arias (here to his few reflective and contemplative soliloquies, always revealing of themes and characters). Above all, there are the complex and varied ways that the music heightens the dramatic effects of the libretto through reinforcing the expressed emotions or revealing deeper contrasting feelings. Add to this finally the visual dimension in set and costume design and stage direction. We cannot help but be fully engaged on every subjective level, absorbed fully in the world of this opera, in appreciating this scene.

One might object at this point that any opera aria will contain similarly complex sets of relations, so that according to the present thesis, all arias should be equally good. The objection is misplaced. The relations in question must be such as to inform our experience of the pieces, making each experienced element cognitively and affectively rich. Just as, on the most basic level, not all notes in purported melodies encourage us to relate them satisfyingly in our experience so as to perceive each naturally in terms of the others, so not all vocal lines relate interestingly to their accompaniments or to the emotions expressed by their texts and so on. It takes a composer of the stature of the mature Verdi to make all these connections significant enough to engage us in their grasp and appreciation.

Structurally similar and equally congenial examples can be provided from the genre of narrative painting: religious, historical, or mythological. Consider as one example an early painting of Poussin's, *Cephalus and Aurora* (see Figure 5.2). We may begin here with sensuous and formal elements, as these form significant internal relations: the warm, Titianesque colors and female flesh tones, punctuated by primary red and blue; the movement of Cephalus toward the center, offset by the thrust to the right of the putti, one of whom holds the portrait up toward Cephalus, and the emptiness of the center itself. These elements become significant on a symbolic level in relation to other works of Poussin: The empty center signifies absence and the separation of red and blue signifies human separation or alienation. Other iconic elements as well, such as the overturned water vessel, reappear in many works. Broader themes emerge here too from appreciation of recurrent themes in Poussin: distances in times and places and in the paintings of this period erotic desire that is rejected, unfulfilled, overcome, or stifled. We appreciate this painting not only by noting similarities with other works in this artist's corpus but by noting contrasts as well.

FIGURE 5.2   Nicolas Poussin, *Cephalus and Aurora*, canvas, reproduced
by courtesy of the Trustees, The National Gallery, London.

The warm colors here stand out in contrast to his later much cooler
palette and still later near-monochromatic paintings. The depiction
of nature here, which reinforces the passions of the mythological
characters, contrasts with his later historical paintings and landscapes, in which the background is classical architecture. The movement toward the center here contrasts with movement away from
the center in many of his history paintings.

   Next we note relations to other artists that clarify themes in this
painting: Titian, from whom Poussin borrows the highly expressive
pose of Cephalus, echoing the theme of erotic desire, and Rubens,
from whom he probably borrows the picture within a picture
(which here makes the wife of Cephalus present to him but not to us
viewers).[21] The most obviously relevant external relation is to the
text of Ovid, interpreted by Poussin through all the above-men-
tioned visual means. Ovid's theme is reinforced in the painting by
color, movement, gesture, the depiction of nature, the use of pictorial sources, and the device, absent in the text, of the portrait within
the picture. All this informs our perception of the canvas, generating

exceptionally rich and satisfying visual experience. Once more our perceptual (sensual), cognitive, and affective capacities interact in appreciating all those relations that constitute the world of this work.

I will not belabor further the countless examples from similar genres and styles that perfectly illustrate the sort of overarching value that I have been describing. To the extent that other art forms and styles lack some of the representational and expressive elements and relations that characterize the works just described, they may seem more difficult to assimilate to the thesis being offered here. We have previously noted, however, how instrumental music that does not clearly express any ordinary emotions, such as string quartets by Haydn, nevertheless unite sensuous affect with cognitive recognition and expectation and with felt volition in the pursuit of musical goals established in the course of its unfolding complex forms. That such forms and the tonal elements from which they are constructed are so detached and so different from anything we encounter in the everyday world of objects and events enables such works to provide truly other worlds as objects of full engagement. That the material of music is experienced as so immanent and yet so evanescent makes it seem to consist in pure creative force, constituting worlds completely devoid of ordinary objects and so offering escape beyond that available in other art forms.[22]

At the other extreme from the sorts of works cited above, perhaps the most difficult cases here (the seemingly most obvious counterexamples) derive from recent minimalist art, for example, monochromatic paintings or the repeating patterns of early paintings by Frank Stella, some of which seem to have achieved near canonical status. It would be easy to dismiss such works, even those within the accepted canon, as of little value. A theory of aesthetic value must imply some standards and certainly need not endorse every work accepted by the art world. But to dismiss all such works would be false to the experience of at least some that approach minimalism in their formal aspects. I shall briefly discuss some of these and also argue that such defense of other genuinely minimalist works as can and has been made fits the present theory rather than refuting it.

It is first worth reiterating a point from a previous section: that simplicity in formal structure does not necessarily generate simple or uniform aesthetic experience. This may be most obvious in the mature paintings of Mark Rothko. (See Figure 5.3.) They consist of

FIGURE 5.3   Mark Rothko, *Red, Brown, and Black, 1958, oil on* canvas,
8' 10³/₈" × 9' 9 ¹/₄", The Museum of Modern Art, New York, Mrs. Simon
Guggenheim Fund. Photograph ©1995 The Museum of Modern Art, New
York.

horizontal rectangles with blurred edges superimposed on differently colored backgrounds that partially appear through them. The
immediate effect is the appearance of ambiguous objects and spaces,
the former seeming sometimes to float above their backgrounds as
veils behind which forms seem to emerge and fade, the latter seeming flat and deep at the same time. These large and deceptively simple forms have been described as suggesting "cosmic expanses and
spiritual illumination,"[23] probably because of their seeming immate-
riality (therefore spirituality) and equivocality, which make them

seem to escape the spaces that contain them. Light seems to shine through the rectangles, but what lies behind them seems hidden, creating both tension and surface calmness. The large canvases seem to envelop the viewer in their vague glowing (or dark and intriguing) spaces, and the experience of loss of self in prolonged contemplation of them is palpable (and remarked upon by Rothko himself).

Such description cannot substitute for seeing the paintings (reproductions lack the same effects), but it hopefully indicates how rich the experience of these works can be. The lack of defined objects (even abstract ones) and spaces challenges perception, which is at the same time assuaged by the combinations of colors. Despite the apparent simplicity of the rectangular shapes, a viewer must look both through and at them, must compare their colors, textures, sizes, depths, while simultaneously grasping the whole composition. The overall effect is similar, if not to that of richly representational paintings, at least to that of abstract musical works in combining affect, imagination, and cognitive grasp of structure.

Those who disagree with my evaluation of these works will find that the above description does not fit their experience of them, which is likely to be less rich in the sense indicated. Equally noteworthy are the ways critics describe other near-monochromatic paintings that have also entered the modern canon (but that do not have similar effects for me). A painting of Barnett Newman is described (not atypically) as follows:

> Anticipation not only lingers but explodes in the figure of *Dionysus*. In the rich green of this painting, the vertical zips joining heaven and earth become horizontal lines, which, like Mondrian's incomplete square, stretch beyond the canvas to encompass the surrounding world. This Dionysian "image" suggests what Hegel describes as the "bacchanalian revel in which no member is sober."[24]

The painting being described consists of a green background with a thin yellow horizontal line nearly halfway up the canvas and a thicker orange line well above the yellow one (the colors are not quite uniform, as in some other Newman canvases). In praising the work, the critic here notes its sensuous qualities, contrasts its formal characteristics to those of other Newman paintings, likens them to those in earlier works of other artists (Mondrian), and attributes to them a rich symbolic and philosophical significance. (He might also have located the work further within the modern formalist and expressionist history that Newman continued.) All this is intended to inform our perception of this painting. Those like me, for whom such descriptions do not succeed in informing our experience in viewing the work, will not similarly appreciate or evaluate it.

The first genuinely monochromatic paintings to be accepted into the canon were thought by their creator Malevich to express similarly deep spiritual truths and to contain in themselves the negations of much of the past history of art. By negating the world of appearance and its means of representation with which earlier painting had been concerned, Malevich took himself to be engaging the whole being in a journey to a deeper reality, a world of pure feeling[25] from which social reforms in the material world could be launched. What is important here is not whether one can accept Malevich's descriptions of his works, which sometimes seem to border on mad ravings, but that evaluation of a black or white square as a great work of art depends not only on according it a logical place in certain historical sequences but also on being able to respond to it as rich in (negative) aesthetic properties and in symbolism obliquely indicated in those descriptions. Those who respond to it only as black or white paint will dismiss its aesthetic value.

Later monochromatic and minimalist paintings of the 1960s, such as those of Yves Klein and Stella, are quite different, intending no mystical symbolism or deep spiritual truths. They instead bring certain modernist trends to their logical conclusion: the elimination of representation and illusion or depth (by flattening the canvas to eliminate all figure and ground)—the emphasis on the media of painting and on formal purity (here allowing the physical canvas to dictate the form). Stella's repeating patterns can be seen as combining Mondrian's geometrical units with Pollock's unified texture.[26] At the same time, all minimalist works opposed what were perceived as the subjective, romantic, expressivist excesses and painterly techniques of the immediately preceding dominant style of abstract expressionism.

The interest in such canvases lies not only in such historical relations but also in the aesthetic paradoxes and resultant cognitive challenges they can present. A perfectly flat, monochromatic surface whose only form is its material shape appears to be simply a physical object (closing the gap with sculpture as well), as critics and artists at the time were aware. Such objects perhaps raise Danto's philosophical question about the relation of artworks to their material substrates and to ordinary physical things more effectively than do the represented objects of Andy Warhol or Jasper Johns. It is paradoxical first of all that when artworks make the attempt to isolate the essence of painting to its logical conclusion, they seem to cease being artworks or paintings and to become mere physical objects. Of course, if they are taken thus to symbolize physical objecthood or the resistance of the physical world, then they are taken to be more than physical objects, and so the attempt to symbolize in this way by becoming mere physical objects must fail (another paradox).[27]

Defenses of such works seek to compensate for the lack of formal content by such interpretive activity and philosophical content. Challenges to cognitive activity substitute for perceptual challenges. But from the point of view of the theory of aesthetic value defended here, the crucial evaluative question for these minimalist works is whether such interpretations can inform our experience in viewing them. If not, then they are bad (because they are obscure) philosophy rather than good art. Defenders also attribute a kind of intensity in the experience of these works based on the fact that all their aesthetically relevant properties (and these include all their material properties, as is not the case in traditional painting) are grasped at once. Such defense again fits the thesis of this section.

These works, in extending and negating different parts of the artistic tradition, present enough to perception and cognition to be classified as art under an evaluative concept. For me, they nevertheless remain external objects in their viewing, not alternative worlds in which we can lose ourselves. Indeed, this may have been part of their intent. Similarly, although they cannot be classified as great works according to the present theory, in attacking romantic conceptions, symbolizing the "death of the artist" and the interpretive power of the critic, they attacked the notion of a great work or masterpiece as well. A theory of value or evaluation that seeks first to capture what great works have in common is unlikely to be sympathetic to such intentions.[28] Unlike a definition of art, which perhaps must accommodate all accepted styles if it is to be plausible, an account of value of the sort intended here need not judge all styles positively. It suffices to point out again that those who do judge these works positively and offer reasons for their judgments assimilate the paintings' effects on us and our reactions to them to those produced by other works that are evaluated positively by our criteria.

Of Time and Taste

I have discussed three ways of evaluating a work of art: (1) in terms of the degree to which its strategies satisfy the ideals of the style under the constraints of which it is produced; (2) in terms of its importance in a historical sequence in which it is placed (determined mainly by the first way of evaluating and by its originality); and (3) simply as an artwork, in terms of its overall effects on us and the degree to which it engages and integrates our mental capacities in appreciating it. In all three cases evaluative judgments seem more secure with the passage of time. First, we can be more secure in retrospect that ideals implicit in or standards applied to various styles will not be better (or worse) satisfied by works as yet to come, changing our evaluations of those being presently judged. Second, a work's place in a plausible historical narrative will be evident only in retrospect, when the narrative can be viewed as complete. Third, a truly great work must engage us not only on initial encounter with it but continually. Initial infatuation with superficially striking features must not fade into boredom with familiarity. In regard to more specific aesthetic properties as well, these can be more readily identified in particular works on the basis of the broader comparisons that the passage of time affords. Fourth, given the view of interpretation defended earlier, the passage of time will make available a greater variety of interpretations that can accentuate different sets of values that may be inherent in a work. This will allow a work that is misunderstood at first to receive a more informed and hence more trustworthy evaluation.

Finally, taste can mature as a result of the broader base of comparison that time affords. A work whose estimation survives changes in tastes is once again more secure in its value. But all these reasons to endorse the test of time (and explanations for its being a legitimate test) can be called into question by a different sort of effect of taste on the construction of art history itself. It is compatible with the earlier claim that stylistic connections among works are real to recognize that current aesthetic preferences among art historians determine which developments are emphasized and hence

which works have their status enhanced by inclusion in art historical narratives.[29] This dependence of art history on taste can result in
artists' reputations rising and falling in roller coaster fashion instead
of showing continuous improvement or decline with the passage of
time. Giotto was considered a great early naturalist during the
Renaissance, a lesser naturalist later, and in the twentieth century a
great formalist precursor of Cézanne. El Greco's fortunes similarly
waxed and waned. More recently and in much shorter time spans
we have seen similar progressions in taste for the works of Dali and
Chagall. Such irregular patterns of evaluation can be predicted
when the same artists are considered in different stylistic contexts
(Giotto as naturalist or formalist, Van Eyck as naturalist or alle-
gorist).

The problem for the test of time posed by these historical patterns can be stated in the form of an apparent inconsistency. If an
artist is rated highly at t_1, considered mediocre at t_2, and considered
first-rate once more at t_3, then it looks inconsistent to hold that the
second judgment is more trustworthy than the first and that the
third is likewise more accurate than the second. The test of time
seems to require this, since it implies that later judgments are to be
preferred to earlier judgments. Yet such claims here would seem to
imply that a low rating is more accurate than a high rating and that
a high rating is more accurate than a low rating. In short the test of
time seems to require linear progressions of evaluations or convergence over time, and yet such convergence may be lacking in real
cases.

At closer look such cases in themselves do not refute the sound-
ness of the test, however. The test of time need not imply that every
later judgment is better than every earlier one—only that judgments tend to become better (tend to approach those of ideal critics) and tend to converge with the passage of time if they are made
with proper care. Careful examination of the explanations for the
cases cited gives further vindication to the proposed criterion. In
the case of Giotto, for example, there are different explanations for
the fall and then the much later rise in his reputation. Both sorts of
explanation were discussed in the previous chapter. The first appeals to the change in standards for naturalistic or realistic depiction in the Renaissance and after, such that Giotto's paintings
looked strikingly lifelike when he painted them but much less so
later on. We noted above that in the face of such changing standards

with the emergence of later styles, critics can stabilize their evaluations by relativizing them to the particular styles of the works being judged. Giotto remains a great naturalist in relation to the fourteenth-century context in which he painted. The passage of time allows for more certain judgment regarding the completion of the strategies, ideals, and constraints of particular styles to which evaluative properties are relativized.

The second explanation appeals to the emergence of new stylistic connections and new art historical narratives (in formalist terms) five centuries after Giotto. Although taste and current fashions in art (in this case the formalism of Cézanne and Clive Bell) play a role in the construction of these narratives, I have maintained that the connections discovered by convincing narratives (I take no stand here on the classification of Giotto[30]) remain secure once established. Such connections may take much time to emerge, as we see in this case, but once made by art historians with certain tastes, they can secure a place in history for artists and their works that remains from then on independent of changing tastes for styles. Again the test of time, if applied over sufficiently long spans, is vindicated.

The effect of taste on the third way of evaluating artworks may be more troubling here. Changing tastes for styles can in themselves cause the overall effects of works on groups of knowledgeable critics at particular times to fluctuate. In admitting that taste can differ even at the highest level among ideal critics, we also admit that there is no one correct evaluation for works of art. Thus it should not surprise us that the test of time will not reveal the single correct evaluation. Correct evaluations by real critics are those that would be shared by ideal critics, who apprehend all the relevant relational properties of the works and who generally share their tastes. The judgments of even ideal critics can differ, but it is crucial to point out at the same time that the tastes of real people can mature and improve. That they tend to do so over time with increased exposure to a variety of works is a final reason why the test of time is applicable not only on the grand historical and social scale but on the individual level as well.

Our final task is to defend this claim that taste can and does improve and to defend the more basic proposition that it implies: that some tastes (and correlatively some genres of art) are better than others. Such claims are questioned by Marxist and some pragmatist aestheticians for whom differentiations among tastes are groundless ploys by elitist groups to maintain their favored social positions. We must also be wary that in judging some tastes to be bad we are not simply measuring distance from our own taste. If either skeptical alternative were true, then aesthetic education that is aimed at improving taste would be called into question as well. A successful argument that they are not true requires finding some criterion by which we can differentiate good taste from bad taste and hence differentiate among types of works as well.

Perhaps the strongest criterion would be a simple extension of Mill's famous suggestion for distinguishing among higher and lower pleasures: that those who have experienced both sorts prefer the former.[31] Unfortunately, Mill's claim is not borne out by experience together with our intuitive differentiations, either in the realm of pleasure or in the narrower realm of taste. My own son, together with many other well brought up teenagers, has been exposed from an early age to symphonic music and opera. Although he does not dislike listening to them, he continues to prefer rock. We must seek more complex and perhaps less conclusive criteria. A weaker test than Mill's, but one that is more plausible, exploits the fact that when taste does change or mature, it tends to do so in particular directions. Few people begin with a preference for Wagner or Mozart and mature to prefer rock or country music. Few begin with a preference for Turner and Constable and come to prefer Florida seascapes and landscapes. Here better taste is more mature taste. Of course, if we define it simply in that way, then we cannot use the fact that taste tends to improve with age as support for the test of time, as previously suggested. Fortunately, whereas the typical direction of change may provide one criterion for distinguishing among tastes, it need not be part of an analysis or definition of good taste.

Before proceeding to that analysis, we may note one further test for distinguishing good taste from bad suggested by the test of direction of change and mentioned much earlier (Chapter 2, under the heading "Realism"). This is to collect works that tend to become preferred by those with mature or experienced taste in each genre and see whether they can be distinguished from lesser works in their categories according to characteristics they share. If so, and if certain genres are themselves richer in those characteristics, then we have another way to compare categories of art and, derivatively, tastes among those categories. Of course, if we could in this way find objective properties that preferred works share, then we could derive principles of the strong kind for evaluating artworks. I have argued at length that there are no such principles. But once more the absence of such principles leaves open the possibility of characterizing better works across genres in terms of their common effects on us (other than the fact that we find them better or more interesting). Having made that distinction, we could then distinguish better tastes in terms of preferring works that relate to us in those ways.

My prediction for the outcome of such an experiment is that it would support the sort of account of superior art defended in the previous section. Within each genre, works tend to become preferred that are more challenging and integrating of all our perceptual, affective, and cognitive capacities, that are rich in internal and/or external relations that make experience of them rich and intense, that are less predictable and immediate in their gratifications. In the realm of music, for example, the prediction is that the same sort of differences between classical and more popular forms—richness of perceivable relational properties for each segment along with tightness of logical progressions; the fact that musical goals are not too obviously or too easily reached; the presence of diversions, prolongations, and deviations from the immediate fulfillment of expectations—also distinguish better popular music from worse.[32] In literature, the best of popular detective fiction, for example, Agatha Christie's *And Then There Were None*, contains in comparison to other works in that genre the same kinds of characteristics—richness and economy of psychological characterization, ingenuity and logical progression of plot in relation to characters, affective atmosphere in relation to setting and character, and so on—that distinguishes more serious literature from most more popular literature.

Those with better taste prefer works that are more challenging and engaging in these ways (not necessarily those that are formally more complex). This nutshell characterization is supported also by the ways we tend to differentiate among tastes in other areas as well: in dress, home decoration, friends, entertainment, and so on. Bad taste is superficial, easily won over by the eye-catching first glance or fast impression, impressed by the garish and moved by the sentimental or maudlin. Good taste is more discriminating, both among and within objects, and is often based on appreciation of less easily perceived, more understated, but more durably significant traits.

These differences in taste are real, although they may depend more on education than on overall intelligence. In maintaining their reality, we need not overstate their importance. They are much less tied to being morally better or worse than some have maintained. As argued earlier, the degree to which avoiding immorality requires the sorts of fine discriminations that good taste involves is highly debatable, and those trained to make such discriminations in the social sphere may use them as much to avoid responsibility as to fulfill it.

The recognition of that fact eliminates one purported reason for supporting aesthetic education as the means to improve taste. Real distinctions among better and worse taste are necessary to a justification for such aesthetic education, but they are not sufficient. The question remains: Wherein lies the value of training students to have better taste in art? Another answer to this question appeals to the general development of cognitive capacities allegedly facilitated by learning to be discriminating among and within artworks. However, even granting the claim that such learning generalizes, the extent to which it does would need to be measured in this context against the effects of more direct training of reasoning abilities, through mathematics or logic, for example.

A more straightforward answer appeals simply to the great pleasure to be derived from being able to appreciate fine artworks, making students' lives more enjoyable when they have acquired this ability. But it is questionable again whether a person's overall aesthetically derived pleasure increases when she is trained to appreciate the more serious as opposed to the more popular art forms. It is questionable because, for example, those trained in the appreciation of classical music and jazz are likely to derive less pleasure than do others from listening to the simpler kinds of rock and country music. How this trades off in terms of overall quantity of aesthetic pleasure seems at best indeterminate. Certainly many devotees of the popular forms are as ardent in their pursuit of its enjoyments as are classical music lovers.

What is needed here is precisely Mill's distinction between qualities, or I would say depth, of pleasure as opposed to quantity of pleasure. Fine art offers a deeper sort of pleasure than do the more popular forms of entertainment, and it is to make such deeply rewarding experience available to students that we offer them aesthetic education. In order for conceptual knowledge gained through such education to enhance the appreciation and enjoyment

of art, one must reach the level of analytic ability and familiarity
with particular kinds of works at which one's knowledge of the
forms, conventions, and relevant history can inform and guide
one's perceptions without intruding into awareness and so alienat-
ing that awareness from the works themselves. But this level can be
achieved with sufficient training and practice, so that what may
block aesthetic enjoyment at first may later enhance it. One who
must concentrate on hearing the variations on a theme may not enjoy the piece as much as the naive listener who does not even know
that they are variations. But one who can hear them right off as
variations will better appreciate their subtlety and ingenuity, and
this appreciation is itself part of a deeper enjoyment.

As argued, we cannot distinguish qualitatively among sorts of
enjoyment in the way Mill proposed (according to the preferences
of those who have experienced both sorts). We must do so again
along the lines we used to distinguish fine artworks from lesser objects of contemplation. Pleasures are deeper in this sense when they
result from meeting challenges and when they involve cognitive capacities as well as sensation and feeling. More superficial pleasures
are "mindless" and escapist in the sense of escape from vigorous
mental activities. Pleasures that derive from the satisfying engagement of all our mental capacities operating together are more
deeply or thoroughly satisfying, and it is these kinds of pleasures
that appreciating fine art affords. Thus the most plausible justification for education in the arts requires appeal to the sort of theory of
aesthetic value here proposed and hence gives yet additional support for that theory.

Aesthetic education does not result in and should not aim at total convergence of evaluation or aesthetic judgment. Those who become most sensitive to certain kinds of aesthetic value may necessarily (because of human limitations) be less sensitive to those
yielded by other styles or genres. That is one reason why, as maintained throughout, we must relativize aesthetic judgments to ideal
(but still human) critics who share tastes. When real people who
seem to have similar taste disagree about a particular work, it is relevant to ask whether the disagreement reveals a difference in (fully
developed) taste or whether one party to the dispute is simply mistaken about the work (his judgment would not be shared by an
ideal critic with generally similar taste). To answer that question, we

role of time – a test
tastes compare over time

better taste = more mature taste

would need to find out whether they agree in their interpretations
of the work (if not, whether they are aware of the alternative interpretations) and, more important, whether they are taking account
of the same base aesthetic properties and relations. We can demand
of ideal critics only that they be sensitive to all the base properties
that can contribute to the aesthetic value of a work, not that they
actually value them.

no universal principles
linking aesthetic properties + overall value
linking base properties + aesthetic properties

style/genre relative

taste

art works derive their value
from the way their objective
properties interact + relate to
each other

ideal critics with similar taste

works are better the more they
enjoy us fully, perceptually,
cognitively + affectively

art work as alternative world
with its own space + time
with its own demands + pull on us
exclusivity (pull us out of ordinary world)

*pleasurable
attending
deeper pleasure*

NOTES

Chapter 1

1. George Dickie, *Art and the Aesthetic: An Institutional Analysis* (Ithaca: Cornell University Press, 1974).

2. Jerrold Levinson, "Defining Art Historically," *British Journal of Aesthetics* 19 (1979):232–250.

3. See, for example, Plato, *The Republic*, Allan Bloom trans. (New York: Basic Books, 1968); Leo Tolstoy, *What Is Art?* A. Maude, trans. (Indianapolis, Ind.: Hackett, 1960); Clive Bell, *Art* (London: Chatto and Windus, 1914). An exception to the predominant analytical definitions in this regard is Monroe Beardsley, *Aesthetics* (Indianapolis, Ind.: Hackett, 1981).

4. Tolstoy, *What Is Art?*

5. Bell, *Art.*

6. Nelson Goodman, *The Languages of Art* (Indianapolis, Ind.: Bobbs-Merrill, 1968).

7. Francis Hutcheson, *An Inquiry into the Original of Our Ideas of Beauty and Virtue* (New York: Garland, 1971).

8. I emphasize the value of great works throughout the ensuing discussion partly because it seems easiest to grasp the nature of aesthetic value from instances in which it is most clearly instantiated. Although this entire category has come under attack of late, its defense in this book consists precisely in the specification of a kind of value that such works share.

9. See R. G. Collingwood, *The Principles of Art* (Oxford: Clarendon Press, 1938).

10. Immanuel Kant, *Critique of Judgment*, W. S. Pluhar, trans. (Indianapolis, Ind.: Hackett, 1987).

11. John Dewey, *Art as Experience* (New York: Capricorn, 1958), p. 117.

12. Ibid., p. 256.

13. See, for example, Pierre Bourdieu, *Distinction: A Social Critique of the Judgment of Taste*, R. Nice, trans. (Cambridge: Harvard University Press, 1984).

Chapter 2

1. Monroe Beardsley, *Aesthetics* (Indianapolis, Ind.: Hackett, 1981), pp. xxviii–xxix.

2. Frank Sibley, "A Contemporary Theory of Aesthetic Qualities: Aesthetic Concepts," *Philosophical Review* 68 (1959), p. 421.

3. Compare Francis Sparshott, *The Theory of the Arts* (Princeton: Princeton University Press, 1982), p. 478.

4. Francis Hutcheson, *An Inquiry into the Original of Our Ideas of Beauty and Virtue* (New York: Garland, 1971), Section 2.

5. Guy Sircello, *A New Theory of Beauty* (Princeton: Princeton University Press, 1975).

6. These conditions may not actually be met. See A. Goldman, *Empirical Knowledge* (Berkeley: University of California Press, 1988), pp. 281–288.

7. Eddy Zemach, "Real Beauty," *Midwest Studies in Philosophy* 16 (1991):249–265.

8. I shall argue in a later chapter that uses of the same evaluative terms do not always express the same responses. But it is sufficient for stable meaning that we associate these terms with a normal expressive function.

9. I owe this point to Stephen Davies.

10. Zemach, *Real Beauty*, pp. 260–261.

11. Goldman, *Empirical Knowledge*, ch. 9.

12. Beardsley, *Aesthetics*, pp. 462–463.

13. Goldman, *Empirical Knowledge*, ch. 13.

14. But we must be cautious in such claims. See also Alan Goldman, "Natural Selection, Justification, and Inference to the Best Explanation," in *Evolution, Cognition, and Realism*, ed. N. Rescher (Lanham, Md.: University Press of America, 1990).

15. This point is made by John Bender, "Supervenience and the Justification of Aesthetic Judgements," *Journal of Aesthetics and Art Criticism* 46 (1987):31–40.

Chapter 3

1. This claim will be further qualified later, when it will be noted that these qualities can alter when in the context of a representation, for example.

2. Leo Tolstoy, *What Is Art?* A. Maude, trans. (Indianapolis, Ind.: Hackett, 1960).

3. See Aaron Ridley, "Pitiful Responses to Music," *British Journal of Aesthetics* 33 (1993):72–74.

4. Compare John Hospers, "The Concept of Artistic Expression," *Proceedings of the Aristotelian Society* 55 (1954–1955), p. 325; also Alan Tormey, *The Concept of Expression* (Princeton: Princeton University Press, 1971), p. 105.

5. Peter Kivy, *Sound Sentiment* (Philadelphia: Temple University Press, 1989), p. 23.

6. Compare Leonard Meyer, *Music, the Arts, and Ideas* (Chicago: University of Chicago Press, 1967), p. 33.

7. Peter Kivy, *Music Alone* (Ithaca: Cornell University Press, 1990), p. 153.

8. The latter point is made first by Eduard Hanslick, *On the Musically Beautiful*, G. Payzant, trans. (Indianapolis, Ind.: Hackett, 1986), p. 9.

9. Kivy, *Music Alone*, ch. 8.

10. The objection is raised by Francis Sparshott, *The Theory of the Arts* (Princeton: Princeton University Press, 1982), p. 219.

11. Kivy, *Sound Sentiment*, p. 58.

12. Compare Stephen Davies, *Musical Meaning and Expression* (Ithaca: Cornell University Press, 1994), pp. 304–305. Our similar criticisms of Kivy were developed independently.

13. Compare Colin Radford, "Emotions in Music: A Reply to the Cognitivists," *Journal of Aesthetics and Art Criticism* 47 (1989), p. 72; also Davies, *Musical Meaning and Expression*, pp. 286–287.

14. Kivy, "Auditor's Emotions: Contentions, Concessions and Compromise," *Journal of Aesthetics and Art Criticism* 51 (1993), p. 2.

15. Kendall Walton, *Mimesis as Make-Believe* (Cambridge: Harvard University Press, 1990), ch. 7.

16. Ibid., p. 336.

17. Kivy, "Auditor's Emotions," p. 10.

18. For recent arguments incorporating many of these claims, see Jerrold Levinson, "Music and Negative Emotion," in *Music, Art, and Metaphysics* (Ithaca: Cornell University Press, 1990).

19. I have treated these topics in *Empirical Knowledge* (Berkeley: University of California Press, 1988).

20. Plato, *The Republic*, Allan Bloom, trans. (New York: Basic Books, 1968), p. 598b.

21. Nelson Goodman, "Reality Remade," in *Languages of Art* (Indianapolis, Ind.: Hackett, 1976).

22. Flint Schier, *Deeper into Pictures* (Cambridge: Cambridge University Press, 1986), p. 44.

23. Schier denies this (ibid., p. 187), arguing that it presupposes a homunculus in the mind who must note the resemblances before the recognitional ability in question can be triggered. But this silly view of perceptual processing is not presupposed here any more than in any appeal to visual processing and recognition via visual cues.

24. See Richard Wollheim, *Painting as an Art* (Princeton: Princeton University Press, 1987), p. 48. Wollheim combines this seeing-in requirement with an intentional criterion.

25. Walton, *Mimesis*, pp. 294, 297.

26. See Christopher Peacocke, "Depiction," *Philosophical Review* 96 (1987):383–410.

27. Compare K. Neander, "Pictorial Representation: A Matter of Resemblance," *British Journal of Aesthetics* 27 (1987):213–226.

28. See Schier, *Deeper into Pictures*, p. 134.

29. See Ernst Gombrich, *Art and Illusion* (New York: Pantheon, 1960).

30. See John Hyman, "Perspective," in *A Companion to Aesthetics*, ed. David Cooper (Oxford: Blackwell, 1992).

31. See Norman Bryson, *Looking at the Overlooked* (Cambridge: Harvard University Press, 1990), p. 61.

32. Nelson Goodman, *Languages of Art* (Indianapolis, Ind.: Bobbs-Merrill, 1968), pp. 52–57.

33. Ibid., p. 260.

34. Ibid., pp. 7–9.

35. For a typical collection of such experimental results, see M. D. Vernon, ed., *Experiments in Visual Perception* (Baltimore: Penguin, 1968). As in philosophy, it is clear from the literature of psychology that highly counterintuitive theoretical claims make the biggest splash, especially if some ingeniously concocted empirical support can be found for them.

36. Goodman, *Languages of Art*, p. 260.

37. See, for example, Ivo Kohler, *The Formation and Transformation of the Perceptual World* (New York: International Universities Press, 1964); and James Taylor, *The Behavioral Basis of Perception* (New Haven: Yale University Press, 1962).

38. Walton, *Mimesis*, p. 34.

39. To be fair to Walton, he does not pretend to offer a theory of aesthetic value for representational paintings in his general theory of representation.

40. For expansion on many of these points, see Walter Abell, *Representation and Form* (Westport, Conn.: Greenwood, 1971).

41. For expansion on these very brief descriptions, see Meyer, *Music, the Arts, and Ideas*; also his *Explaining Music* (Berkeley: University of California Press, 1973).

42. For an excellent description of the form and its variations, see Charles Rosen, *Sonata Forms* (New York: W. W. Norton, 1980).

43. John Dewey, *Art as Experience* (New York: Capricorn, 1958), pp. 107, 117–118, 137.

44. Aristotle, *Poetics*, in *The Basic Works of Aristotle*, ed. Richard McKeon (New York: Random House, 1941), pp. 1465, 1469–1470.

45. Charles Rosen, *The Classical Style* (New York: W. W. Norton, 1972), p. 29.

Chapter 4

1. See, for example, Robert J. Matthews, "Describing and Interpreting a Work of Art," *Journal of Aesthetics and Art Criticism* 36 (1977):5–14; Annette Barnes, *On Interpretation* (Oxford: Basil Blackwell, 1988), chs. 2, 3.

2. Arthur Danto, *The Transfiguration of the Commonplace* (Cambridge: Harvard University Press, 1981), ch. 1.

3. Richard Shusterman, "Interpretation, Intention, and Truth," *Journal of Aesthetics and Art Criticism* 46 (1987–1988), p. 403.

4. This analogy was suggested by Jerrold Levinson in "Performance Versus Critical Interpretation in Music," pp. 33–60 in *The Interpretation of Music: Philosophical Essays,* ed. Michael Krausz (Oxford: Clarendon Press, 1993).

5. Levinson once more makes a similar point; see ibid.

6. Compare Daniel O. Nathan, "Irony, Metaphor, and the Problem of Intention," in *Intention and Interpretation,* ed. Gary Iseminger (Philadelphia: Temple University Press, 1992), pp. 197–198.

7. A few similar accounts have been suggested in the literature. One is P. D. Juhl, "The Appeal to the Text," *Journal of Aesthetics and Art Criticism* 36 (1978):277–287. Juhl suggests that interpretations explain texts by appealing to authors' intentions to fulfill the value criteria of coherence and complexity. My account is not limited to appeal to authors' intentions, and it recognizes diverse sources of artistic value. A second is Jeffrey Olin, "Theories, Interpretations, and Aesthetic Qualities," *Journal of Aesthetics and Art Criticism* 35 (1977):425–431. He sees interpretations as explanatory theories that seek to unify works. I see unity as at most one formal aesthetic value, and my account applies to parts or elements of works as well. A third is Ronald Dworkin, "Law as Interpretation," *Critical Inquiry* 9 (1982):179–200. Dworkin sees as a goal of interpretation making a text as aesthetically good as it can be. I agree (taking 'aesthetic' in a broad sense), and my account is closest to his. But I emphasize that the diverse sources of aesthetic value imply incompatible but equally acceptable interpretations of the same works, an implication inimical to Dworkin's general program.

8. See, for example, Monroe Beardsley, *The Possibility of Criticism* (Detroit: Wayne State University Press, 1970); E. D. Hirsch, *Validity in Interpretation* (New Haven: Yale University Press, 1967); Stanley Fish, *Is There a Text in This Class?* (Cambridge: Harvard University Press, 1980).

9. Beardsley, *The Possibility of Criticism,* pp. 38–39.

10. I have treated them in *Empirical Knowledge* (Berkeley: University of California Press, 1988).

11. See especially Fish, *Is There a Text in This Class?*

12. Ibid., p. 368.

13. Ibid., e.g., p. 318.

14. Ibid., p. 347.

15. E. D. Hirsch, *Validity in Interpretation* (New Haven: Yale University Press, 1967), chs. 1, 2.

16. Ibid., p. 27.

17. Noël Carroll, "Art, Intention, and Conversation," in *Intention and Interpretation*, ed. Gary Iseminger (Philadelphia: Temple University Press, 1992).

18. Ibid., pp. 119–120.

19. See William Tolhurst, "On What a Text Is and How It Means," *British Journal of Aesthetics* 19 (1979):3–14; Jerrold Levinson, "Intention and Interpretation: A Last Look," in *Intention and Interpretation*.

20. Compare R. Stecker, "The Role of Intention and Convention in Interpreting Artworks," *Southern Journal of Philosophy* 31 (1994):471–489.

21. David Lewis, "Truth in Fiction," in *Philosophical Papers*, vol. 1 (New York: Oxford University Press, 1983), p. 270.

22. Nicholas Wolterstorff, *Works and Worlds of Art* (Oxford: Clarendon Press, 1980), p. 120.

23. Kendall Walton, *Mimesis as Make-Believe* (Cambridge: Harvard University Press, 1990), p. 169.

24. Ibid., p. 185.

25. Gregory Currie, *The Nature of Fiction* (Cambridge: Cambridge University Press, 1990), ch. 2.

26. Anita Silvers, "The Story of Art Is the Test of Time," *Journal of Aesthetics and Art Criticism* 49 (1991), p. 217.

27. Arthur Danto calls properties that can be known only in retrospect, after further developments, "narrative properties." See his *Narration and Knowledge* (New York: Columbia University Press, 1985), chs. 8, 15.

28. The account of style thus far is similar to that provided by James Carney in several articles. See, for example, "The Style Theory of Art," *Pacific Philosophical Quarterly* 72 (1991), p. 274.

29. For an excellent account of such shifts, see David Carrier, *Principles of Art History Writing* (University Park: Pennsylvania State University Press, 1991).

30. See Richard Wollheim, *Painting as an Art* (Princeton: Princeton University Press, 1987), p. 26.

31. Arthur Danto, "Narrative and Style," *Journal of Aesthetics and Art Criticism* 49 (1991), p. 205.

Chapter 5

1. Stephen Davies claims that deductive evaluative arguments are possible in just this way. See "Replies to Arguments Suggesting that Critics' Strong Evaluations Could Not Be Soundly Deduced," *Grazer Philosophische Studien* 38 (1990):157–175.

2. For the latter notion, see Judith Thomson, "Goodness and Utilitarianism," *Proceedings and Addresses of the American Philosophical Association* 67, no. 2 (1993):145–159.

3. Frank Sibley, "A Contemporary Theory of Aesthetic Qualities: Aesthetic Concepts," *Philosophical Review* 68 (1959):421–450.

4. See William Lycan and Peter Machamer, "A Theory of Critical Reasons," in *Language and Aesthetics,* ed. B. R. Tilghman (Lawrence: University Press of Kansas, 1973).

5. Alan Goldman, *Empirical Knowledge* (Berkeley: University of California Press, 1988), ch. 14.

6. David Pole, "Art and Generality," in *Aesthetics, Form and Emotion* (New York: St. Martin's, 1983).

7. Monroe Beardsley, *Aesthetics* (Indianapolis, Ind.: Hackett, 1981), p. 529.

8. Ibid., for example, p. 462.

9. George Dickie, *Evaluating Art* (Philadelphia: Temple University Press, 1988) pp. 86–89.

10. The argument for moral relativism is provided in Alan Goldman, *Moral Knowledge* (London: Routledge, 1988), chs. 2, 4.

11. We can, however, compare actual frameworks to see if they might be embraced by ideal judges, and here the constraints are more stringent than in the case of ideal aesthetic evaluators, as noted below.

12. See, for example, Mary Mothersill, *Beauty Restored* (Oxford: Clarendon Press, 1984), pp. 170–171.

13. Given that ideal judges must be coherent in this way, judgments analyzed as above come out true when they are coherent. The other features of ideal judges determine the class of settled judgments with which others must cohere.

14. See Goldman, *Moral Knowledge*, chs. 4–5.

15. See Martha Nussbaum, *Love's Knowledge* (Oxford: Oxford University Press, 1990).

16. In the case of music, the very material from which works are constructed is otherworldly. Sounds are first of all detachable from the objects that produce them, and musical tones are doubly removed from environmental objects in not being natural sounds. See Edward Lippman, *A Humanistic Philosophy of Music* (New York: New York University Press, 1977), ch. 2.

17. The space and time referred to here is not represented space and time, since what is represented in representational works is normally real space and time.

18. See Arthur Danto, *The Philosophical Disenfranchisement of Art* (New York: Columbia University Press, 1986).

19. See Kendall Walton, *Mimesis as Make-Believe* (Cambridge: Harvard University Press, 1990).

20. See, for example, Kathleen Higgins, *The Music of Our Lives* (Philadelphia: Temple University Press, 1991).

21. See Richard Wollheim, *Painting as an Art* (Princeton: Princeton University Press, 1987), pp. 198–199, as well as the evidence that he cites. See also David Carrier, *Poussin's Paintings* (University Park: Pennsylvania State University Press, 1993), p. 137; Anthony Blunt, *Nicolas Poussin* (New York: Pantheon, 1967), pp. 79, 124.

22. This is not to make any claim of general superiority for the art form. The more purely "other" the world of an artwork is, the less it lends itself to comparison with the real world and the values to be derived therefrom.

23. James E.B. Breslin, *Mark Rothko* (Chicago: University of Chicago Press, 1993), p. 274.

24. Mark C. Taylor, *Disfiguring* (Chicago: University of Chicago Press, 1992), p. 92.

25. Kazimir Malevich, *The Non-objective World* (Chicago: Paul Theobald, 1959).

26. Frances Colpitt, *Minimal Art: The Critical Perspective* (Ann Arbor, Mich.: UMI Research Press, 1990), p. 60.

27. Compare Arthur Danto, *The Transfiguration of the Commonplace* (Cambridge: Harvard University Press, 1981), p. 159.

28. I have said nothing explicit since the Introduction about the claim that the notion of greatness in art only reflects and reinforces the power of privileged classes within society. There I noted only that the disagreements within elite classes and the enormous popular appeal of many great works make this claim at least empirically suspect. The further defense of my emphasis on these works lay in the development of the thesis that they indeed share certain sorts of effects that give them greater value and possibilities for appreciation than lesser works.

29. See Anita Silvers, "The Story of Art Is the Test of Time," *Journal of Aesthetics and Art Criticism* 49 (1991):211–224.

30. See Clive Bell, *Art* (New York: Frederick Stokes, 1914), p. 147.

31. J. S. Mill, *Utilitarianism* (Indianapolis, Ind.: Bobbs-Merrill, 1957), p. 12.

32. The suggested evaluation here is of popular music as music alone. It is compatible, however, with the recognition that much rock music, for example, is better when seen in performance than when only heard.

Abell, Walter, *Representation and Form*. Westport, Conn.: Greenwood, 1971.

Aristotle, *Poetics*, in *The Basic Works of Aristotle*, ed. Richard McKeon. New York: Random House, 1941.

Barnes, Annette, *On Interpretation*. Oxford: Blackwell, 1988.

Beardsley, Monroe, *Aesthetics*. Indianapolis: Hackett, 1981.

———, *The Possibility of Criticism*. Detroit: Wayne State University Press, 1970.

Bell, Clive, *Art*. New York: Frederick Stokes, 1914.

Bender, John, "Supervenience and the Justification of Aesthetic Judgements," *Journal of Aesthetics and Art Criticism* 46 (1987):31–40.

Blunt, Anthony, *Nicolas Poussin*. New York: Pantheon, 1967.

Bourdieu, Pierre, *Distinction: A Social Critique of the Judgment of Taste*, trans. R. Nice. Cambridge: Harvard University Press, 1984.

Breslin, James, *Mark Rothko*. Chicago: University of Chicago Press, 1993.

Bryson, Norman, *Looking at the Overlooked*. Cambridge: Harvard University Press, 1990.

Carney, James, "The Style Theory of Art," *Pacific Philosophical Quarterly* 72 (1991):272–289.

Carrier, David, *Poussin's Paintings*. University Park: Pennsylvania State University Press, 1993.

———, *Principles of Art History Writing*. University Park: Pennsylvania State University Press, 1991.

Carroll, Noël, "Art, Intention, and Conversation," pp. 97–131 in *Intention and Interpretation*, ed. Gary Iseminger. Philadelphia: Temple University Press, 1992.

Collingwood, R. G., *The Principles of Art*. Oxford: Clarendon Press, 1938.

Colpitt, Frances, *Minimal Art: The Critical Perspective*. Ann Arbor, Mich.: UMI Research Press, 1990.

Currie, Gregory, *The Nature of Fiction*. Cambridge: Cambridge University Press, 1990.

Danto, Arthur, *Narration and Knowledge*. New York: Columbia University Press, 1985.

———, "Narrative and Style," *Journal of Aesthetics and Art Criticism* 49 (1991):201–209.

————, *The Philosophical Disenfranchisement of Art*. New York: Columbia University Press, 1986.

————, *The Transfiguration of the Commonplace*. Cambridge: Harvard University Press, 1981.

Davies, Stephen, *Musical Meaning and Expression*. Ithaca: Cornell University Press, 1994.

————, "Replies to Arguments Suggesting that Critics' Strong Evaluations Could Not Be Soundly Deduced," *Grazer Philosophische Studien* 38 (1990):157–175.

Dewey, John, *Art as Experience*. New York: Capricorn, 1958.

Dickie, George, *Art and the Aesthetic: An Institutional Analysis*. Ithaca: Cornell University Press, 1974.

————, *Evaluating Art*. Philadelphia: Temple University Press, 1988.

Dworkin, Ronald, "Law as Interpretation," *Critical Inquiry* 9 (1982): 179–200.

Fish, Stanley, *Is There a Text in This Class?* Cambridge: Harvard University Press, 1980.

Goldman, Alan, *Empirical Knowledge*. Berkeley: University of California Press, 1988.

————, *Moral Knowledge*. London: Routledge, 1988.

————, "Natural Selection, Justification, and Inference to the Best Explanation," pp. 39–46 in *Evolution, Cognition, and Realism*, ed. N. Rescher. Lanham, Md.: University Press of America, 1990.

Gombrich, Ernst, *Art and Illusion*. New York: Pantheon, 1960.

Goodman, Nelson, *Languages of Art*. Indianapolis: Hackett, 1976.

Hanslick, Eduard, *On the Musically Beautiful*, trans. G. Payzant. Indianapolis: Hackett, 1986.

Higgins, Kathleen, *The Music of Our Lives*. Philadelphia: Temple University Press, 1991.

Hirsch, E. D., *Validity in Interpretation*. New Haven: Yale University Press, 1967.

Hospers, John, "The Concept of Artistic Expression," *Proceedings of the Aristotelian Society* 55 (1954–1955):313–344.

Hutcheson, Francis, *An Inquiry into the Original of Our Ideas of Beauty and Virtue*. New York: Garland, 1971.

Hyman, John, "Perspective," pp. 323–327 in *A Companion to Aesthetics*, ed. David Cooper. Oxford: Blackwell, 1992.

Juhl, P. D., "The Appeal to the Text," *Journal of Aesthetics and Art Criticism* 36 (1978):277–287.

Kant, Immanuel, *Critique of Judgment*, trans. W. S. Pluhar. Indianapolis: Hackett, 1987.

Kivy, Peter, "Auditor's Emotions: Contentions, Concessions and Compromise," *Journal of Aesthetics and Art Criticism* 51 (1993):1–12.

———, *Music Alone*. Ithaca: Cornell University Press, 1990.

———, *Sound Sentiment*. Philadelphia: Temple University Press, 1989.

Kohler, Ivo, *The Formation and Transformation of the Perceptual World*. New York: International Universities Press, 1964.

Levinson, Jerrold, "Defining Art Historically," *British Journal of Aesthetics* 19 (1979):232–250.

———, "Intention and Interpretation: A Last Look," pp. 221–256 in *Intention and Interpretation*, ed. Gary Iseminger. Philadelphia: Temple University Press, 1992.

———, "Music and Negative Emotion," pp. 306–335 in *Music, Art, and Metaphysics*. Ithaca: Cornell University Press, 1994.

———, "Performance Versus Critical Interpretation in Music," pp. 33–60 in *The Interpretation of Music: Philosophical Essays*, ed. Michael Krausz. Oxford: Clarendon Press, 1993.

Lewis, David, "Truth in Fiction," pp. 261–280 in *Philosophical Papers*, vol. 1. New York: Oxford University Press, 1983.

Lippman, Edward, *A Humanistic Philosophy of Music*. New York: New York University Press, 1977.

Lycan, William, and Machamer, Peter, "A Theory of Critical Reasons," pp. 87–112 in *Language and Aesthetics*, ed. B. R. Tilghman. Lawrence: University Press of Kansas, 1973.

Malevich, Kazimir, *The Non-objective World*. Chicago: Paul Theobald, 1959.

Matthews, Robert J., "Describing and Interpreting a Work of Art," *Journal of Aesthetics and Art Criticism* 36 (1977):5–14.

Meyer, Leonard, *Explaining Music*. Berkeley: University of California Press, 1973.

———, *Music, the Arts, and Ideas*. Chicago: University of Chicago Press, 1967.

Mill, J. S., *Utilitarianism*. Indianapolis: Bobbs-Merrill, 1957.

Mothersill, Mary, *Beauty Restored*. Oxford: Clarendon Press, 1984.

Nathan, Daniel O., "Irony, Metaphor, and the Problem of Intention," pp. 183–202 in *Intention and Interpretation*, ed. Gary Iseminger. Philadelphia: Temple University Press, 1992.

Neander, K., "Pictorial Representation: A Matter of Resemblance," *British Journal of Aesthetics* 27 (1987):213–226.

Nussbaum, Martha, *Love's Knowledge*. Oxford: Oxford University Press, 1990.

Olin, Jeffrey, "Theories, Interpretations, and Aesthetic Qualities," *Journal of Aesthetics and Art Criticism* 35 (1977):425–431.

Peacocke, Christopher, "Depiction," *Philosophical Review* 96 (1987): 383–410.

Plato, *Republic*, trans. Allan Bloom. New York: Basic Books, 1968.

Pole, David, "Art and Generality," in *Aesthetics, Form and Emotion*. New York: St. Martin's, 1983.

Radford, Colin, "Emotions in Music: A Reply to the Cognitivists," *Journal of Aesthetics and Art Criticism* 47 (1989): 69–76.

Ridley, Aaron, "Pitiful Responses to Music," *British Journal of Aesthetics* 33 (1993):72–74.

Rosen, Charles, *The Classical Style*. New York: W. W. Norton, 1972.

————, *Sonata Forms*. New York: W. W. Norton, 1980.

Schier, Flint, *Deeper into Pictures*. Cambridge: Cambridge University Press, 1986.

Shusterman, Richard, "Interpretation, Intention, and Truth," *Journal of Aesthetics and Art Criticism* 46 (1987–1988):399–411.

Sibley, Frank, "A Contemporary Theory of Aesthetic Qualities: Aesthetic Concepts," *Philosophical Review* 68 (1959):421–450.

Silvers, Anita, "The Story of Art Is the Test of Time," *Journal of Aesthetics and Art Criticism* 49 (1991):211–224.

Sircello, Guy, *A New Theory of Beauty*. Princeton: Princeton University Press, 1975.

Sparshott, Francis, *A Theory of the Arts*. Princeton: Princeton University Press, 1982.

Stecker, R., "The Role of Intention and Convention in Interpreting Artworks," *Southern Journal of Philosophy* 31 (1994):471–489.

Taylor, James, *The Behavioral Basis of Perception*. New Haven: Yale University Press, 1962.

Taylor, Mark, *Disfiguring*. Chicago: University of Chicago Press, 1992.

Thomson, Judith, "Goodness and Utilitarianism," *Proceedings and Addresses of the American Philosophical Association* 67 (1993): 145–159.

Tolhurst, William, "On What a Text Is and How It Means," *British Journal of Aesthetics* 19 (1979):3–14.

Tolstoy, Leo, *What is Art?* trans. A. Maude. Indianapolis: Hackett, 1960.

Tormey, Alan, *The Concept of Expression*. Princeton: Princeton University Press, 1971.

Vernon, M. D., ed., *Experiments in Visual Perception*. Baltimore: Penguin, 1968.

Walton, Kendall, *Mimesis as Make-Believe*. Cambridge: Harvard University Press, 1990.

Wollheim, Richard, *Painting as an Art*. Princeton: Princeton University Press, 1987.

Wolterstorff, Nicholas, *Works and Worlds of Art*. Oxford: Clarendon, 1980.

Zemach, Eddy, "Real Beauty," *Midwest Studies in Philosophy* 16 (1991):249–265.

ABOUT THE BOOK
AND AUTHOR

At the heart of aesthetics lie fundamental questions about value in art and the objectivity of aesthetic valuation. A theory of aesthetic value must explain how the properties of artworks contribute to the values derived from contemplating and appreciating works of art. When someone passes judgment on a work of art, just what is it that is happening, and how can such judgments be criticized and defended?

In this concise survey, intended for advanced undergraduate students of aesthetics, Alan Goldman focuses on the question of aesthetic value, using many practical examples from painting, music, and literature to make his case. Although he treats a wide variety of views, he argues for a nonrealist view of aesthetic value, showing that the personal element can never be factored out of evaluative aesthetic judgments and explaining why this is so. At the same time, he argues for certain common effects of highly esteemed artworks.

Along the way Goldman considers such key topics as interpretation, representation, expression, and taste. His text will be a valuable contribution to the teaching of aesthetics as well as to the understanding of these topics on the part of students and scholars in philosophy and the arts.

Alan H. Goldman is professor of philosophy at the University of Miami. He is the author of many articles and books on ethics and epistemology, including *Moral Knowledge* and *Empirical Knowledge.* More recently, he has published important papers on aesthetics.

Olin, Jeffrey, 183(n7)
One-many relation, 56
Opera, 86, 105, 155–163
Originality, 114–115, 153, 170
Ovid, 164

Paintings, 38, 43, 46, 63, 64, 96, 119,
    125, 141, 151–152
  abstract, 78–79, 109, 121, 155,
    165–169
  copies of, 18, 41, 49, 65
  elements of, 84, 95
  interpretation of, 101
  minimalist, 109, 165–169
  narrative, 163–165
  as physical objects, 168–169
  representation in, 63, 64–82, 116,
    125. *See also* Representation
  See also individual painters
Paradoxes, 168, 169
Paris, 2
Parmigianino, Girolamo, 77
Perception, 82, 87, 102
  alteration of, 74, 75
  direct, 95, 96
Perspective, 71, 77
Picasso, Pablo, 73, 121
Pity, 54
Plato, 3, 46, 64, 106, 153. *See also*
    Representation, aesthetic value of
Pleasure, 4, 10, 15, 22, 23, 78, 87, 141,
    173
  quality vs. quantity of, 15, 175–176
Pole, David, 139
Political issues, 153–154
Portraiture, 72–73, 77
Poussin, Nicolas, 163–165
Power, 120
Predictability, 147
Psychology, 60, 182(n35)
  perception experiments, 75
  See also Freudianism

Realism (philosophical), 26–39, 43, 108
  degrees of, 38
  scientific, 34–35
Realism (true-to-lifeness), 70–72, 77,
    125, 171

Reality Principle, 118
Red, Brown, and Black (Rothko),
    166(fig.)
Reductionism, 11
Relativism/relativizing, 11, 38, 106,
    120–130, 143, 172, 176. *See also*
    Evaluation, relativizing to tastes
Religion, 4, 155
Renaissance, 71, 119, 171
Renoir, Pierre Auguste, 78
Representation, 3, 4, 8, 45–46, 82, 88,
    99, 116–120, 150
  vs. abstraction, 79
  aesthetic value of, 72–81
  conventions concerning, 66–67, 68,
    69–70, 71, 74
  criteria for, 64–70
  intention to represent, 65, 66–67, 69,
    70
  and other sources of value, 78–81
  See also Depiction; Realism (true-to-
    lifeness); *under* Form; Paintings
Resemblance, 68. *See also under*
    Depiction
Romanticism, 46, 129
Rossini, Gioacchino Antonio, 46, 48
Rothko, Mark, 91, 165–167
Rowen, Charles, 88
Rubens, Peter Paul, 121, 164

Sadness, 54. *See also under* Music
Saint-Saëns, Camille, 29, 33, 37
Salieri, 147
Schönberg, Arnold, 147
Scientific theories, 34–36, 97
Secondary qualities, 21, 39, 44. *See also*
    Colors
Sensitivity, 21, 22, 61, 62, 177
Sensations, 59
Sensuous qualities, 46, 74, 165
Shakespeare, William, 101, 139
Sherlock Holmes, 116, 117, 119
Shier, Flint, 68, 181(n23)
Shusterman, Richard, 96–97
Sibley, Frank, 19, 134–135, 138
Silvers, Anita, 121
Simplicity, 35, 141, 165
Skepticism, 11, 30, 57, 122, 123

Everest 20K at Hotmail.com

1-305-
669-4913